CONTEMPORARY RETELLINGS OF MYTHS

AN APPRAISAL

CONTEMPORARY RETELLINGS OF MYTHS

AN APPRAISAL

Editors

Anuradha

Sanjeev Kumar

AUTHORSPRESS

Worldwide Circulation through Authorspress Global Network
First Published in 2023
by
Authorspress
Q-2A Hauz Khas Enclave, New Delhi-110 016 (India)
Phone: (0) 9818049852
E-mail: authorspressgroup@gmail.com
Website: www.authorspressbooks.com

Contemporary Retellings of Myths: An Appraisal

ISBN 978-93-5529-585-9

Printed in India at Kensington Press

To

Those

Who Created

And

Spread

Myths

Foreword

Mythology in the post-truth world, where people accept arguments based on emotions rather than objective standards for truth, is about drawing parallel with the modern world. Myths are cultural truth and collective unconscious of a community or society; at the same time, political myths are about heroes' projection. They reflect socio-cultural ethos of earlier times and can be used to contextualise the same. Mythology as such is a literary device used to portray contemporary issues and sensibility. As an instrument of change, myths, according to Indian cultural critic Devdutt Pattanaik are core carriers of subversive feelings, protests against injustice and aspirational conjectures of subjugated peoples. Myths as the text to represent subjective truth based on memory and mapping of human mind, turning into a psychological phenomenon.

Epics being the best source for myths offer a sense of discovery and establish cross connections between past and present beyond nationality, race, culture and tradition. The key objectives of studying epics are humanitarian, literary, history, progressive and philosophy. Hence, myths carry the core characteristics of literature i.e. universality.

While tracing a sustained connection between myth and folk, David Myatt says that one of the fundamental aims of the way of the folk is to continue the work of nature by creating better, more advanced, individuals and by creating a better, more advanced, more civilised society for these individuals to live and flourish in. Roland Barthes in his book *Mythologies* (1991) writes that myth is a type of speech (message). The study of this message is mythology. Ferdinand de Saussure took mythology to semiology in terms of studying myth as a category of form and meaning. Barthes further says that myths are the reconciliatory tool between reality and men, description and explanation, object and knowledge.

The book titled, *Contemporary Retellings of Myths: An Appraisal* edited by Anuradha and Sanjeev Kumar is the compendium of chapters on salient aspects of myth and mythology as the social discourse. The eclectic range of topics covered in the book manifest a deep understanding of myth as a socio-literary genre by the editors. The thematic division of the book exhibits its structural appropriacy and relevance of the content vis-à-vis modern context.

The topics discussed in the book range from aesthetics of myths, myths and allusions in contemporary literature, myths and cross-cultural exploration, myth and renewal of faith, myth and superstition, myth as a gateway to intertextuality, myth as reflection of reclaiming the past to myth in postmodern literature, etc.

The book, I am sure, is definitely an invaluable contribution to the existing knowledge on myth and mythology and proves to be an important source of reference for the prospective researchers in this area.

Ravi Bhushan
Professor and Chair, Dept of English
BPS Mahila Vishwavidyalaya
Khanpur Kalan, Sonipat (Haryana)

Preface

Myths have been an indispensable part of any civilisation/nation or community that boasts of being significantly old and carries its cultural heritage from generation to generation. They have been a part of the oral tradition of that society and might have been partly true partly imaginative or purely imaginative. The fact that all mythical stories, until they got written, might have travelled orally for many generations and, consequently, might have got changed or distorted partially or wholly. The origin and authenticity of myths, thus, is debatable and beyond the space and scope of this book and is left on the understanding of the readers.

The great themes of myths include the inception and structure of the universe, and the hidden motifs of life and death. They also talk about gods, goddesses and demons, and other supernatural beings. There are cosmic disasters, and heroes and tricksters as agents of change. There is focus on the body and the soul, and on social order. The list is endless as myths are created from life itself and hence they deal with innumerable aspects of life and, consequently, treat life as a complex phenomenon.

The retelling of myths is in vogue in contemporary times. The resurgence in mythological literature may be because of human tendency to relate himself with gods and goddesses, classical tales having supernatural characters, and myths. Myths and classical tales, one can argue, have been a contested discipline. There is, however, universality of connection and appeal in such myths and classical tales that bind humanity to them and inspire them to choose and follow the right path in life. The truth that myths are stories with "unique universal value," Kavita Kane asserts, is universally acknowledged and treated as such (341). Robert Graves is of the opinion that myths are "seldom simple, and never irresponsible" which highlights the value and significance of myths (8).

The contemporary retellings of myths provide another platform to writers to channelise their creative energy in a contested discipline and rewrite such ancient tales with new flavour and aroma. Writing about myths, Kane maintains, "gave [her] a creative canvas to portray contemporary sensibilities against a backdrop of our epics and ancient texts" (341). Kane and such other writers rewrite the mythical tales not from the traditional point of view or from the perspectives of traditional narrators but from a fresh perspective and from the point of view of the characters who had been ignored, marginalised or *othered* in one way or the other. These retellings or rewritings of myths or ancient tales allow the authors to take liberty with the contents and narration and to allow them make it accessible to people who had already been involved in these myths and classical tales through religious or oral tradition. The process of rewriting the myths, as a matter of fact, offers nuanced, complex portraits of characters and often provides new revelations.

Another significant aspect of retellings of myths is a writer's indifference to the meaning and explanations of the myths retold. Stephen Fry, for instance, asserts, "I am only concerned with 'telling' the stories, not with explaining them or investigating the human truths and psychological insights that may lie behind them. The myths are fascinating enough in all their disturbing, surprising, romantic, comic, tragic, violent, and enchanting detail to stand on their own as stories" (11). At the same time, however, it is also true that myths transmit traditional culture-specific understanding of the universe and hence cannot be ignored or put aside without deducing any meaning relating to life and its complexities. Devdutt Pattanaik argues that a myth "constructs a worldview for a people. It serves as a looking glass through which life comes to order. In other words it constructs a paradigm so that the apparently chaotic world comes to possess a structure" (34).

This anthology of papers attempts to understand myriad strands of myths and their retellings in contemporary times. In "Myth and Post-Truth: Some Conjectures on Connection," Yash Pal and Santosh co-relate myths with post-truth and assert that postmodern politics and media creates their own fluidic sense of reality, thereby creating myths of their own and exerting influence on the psyche of the common man. Both myths and post-truth are antithetical to the common human reason, he asserts, but find home in their story-telling, narrative-generating aspect, thus standing against science, scientific method, critical thinking and moral progress.

Vanya Goyal, in "Disney Animated Adaptations as Modern Mythology and Folklore," studies *Hercules*, *Mulan* and *Moana* and argues that Disney Animation Studio has disneyfied the original stories and disseminates specific cultures or myths among broader public for their interpretation of such cultures and myths. She uses a comparative approach to see the similarities and distinctions between the original stories and their Disney versions to see how the stories, the characters and even settings have been altered to create interest of larger audience.

M. Samadhanam Emimal, in her paper "Eliciting Truth and Social Reality: A Postmodern Critiques on Retold Fairytales" argues that retold fairytales, through their postmodern creativity, promulgate altered dimensions of truth and its functioning. Taking cue from Tanith Lee's *Red as Blood* and Emma Donoghue's *Kissing the Witch,* she asserts that the contemporary retellings of fairytales through postmodern temperament and its narrative nuances express radical notions against the canonised conventions of the classical fairytales. This not only deconstructs the conventional patterns but also reconstructs it to reflect the contemporary sensibility, and hence, eventually altering readers' apprehension and challenges the customary assurance inferred through the classical narratives.

Virender Pal, in his paper "Rewriting the Ancient Epics for Propagating Ideology: A Study of Volga's *The Liberation of Sita,*" examines the use of mythical stories by Volga to underline and assert her take on feminism. In twisting the incidents as depicted in *Ramayana,* the writer uses her artistic liberty but contradicts herself at places. He asserts that Volga has rewritten the stories from *Ramayana* to propound a particular ideology. The ideology remains but the stories lose themselves in that attempt. Instead of intertwining her ideology in the stories, Pal maintains, she lets her ideology overpower the stories and ultimately, bland ideology remains.

In "Dialectics of Mythological Echoes in Select Stories of Mahasweta Devi," Poonam Chaudhary asserts that the writer is committed to restoring human values through her stories rooted in Indian mythology. Stories like "Draupadi," "Dhouli," "Sanichari" and "Fairy Tale of Rajbhasha" present her deepest concerns about the retrograde conventionalities of modern society that make it a pull work of exploitative mechanism. The writer is motivated by a sense of history, Chaudhary maintains, in depicting the life-like situations in contemporary society.

Thejimol George, in her paper "Untold Sagas of Kunti's Motherhood: Rewriting the Myth in Tagore's *Karna Kunti Samvad* and G. Sankara Pillai's *Wings Flapping Somewhere,*" explores the mythical character of Kunti and finds it different from Vyasa's Kunti as depicted in the epic *Mahabharata.* Both the writers, according to George, perceived Kunti as a human being with her flaws and limitations which, however, is different from the epic. Her deconstructive reading of the two texts unfolds the fissures and gaps in the myths and reveals the bond between the fostered son Karna and a long-lost mother in these tales of motherhood.

In "Myths, Women and Subalternity: An Examination of Kavita Kane's *Lanka Princes,*" Anshuman highlights how the novelist has presented Meenakshi aka Surpanakha not as a furious and ravenous female demon but as an intelligent, sharp-witted, bold and fiery woman yearning for love, happiness and acceptance. Though misinterpreted, misunderstood and mistreated, Surpanakha has been reduced to a compromised status in the mythological tale and has been nullified in several ways by the patriarchal society. Kane's retold tale of Surpanakha reveals her pain, trauma, loss, humiliation and marginalization to show the other, hidden side of her life.

"Mythicizing 'the Brahminical Knowledge' through Myth in Girish Karnad's *The Fire and the Rain*" by Shobha R. investigates the reinterpretation and recreation of myth of Yavakari and asserts that a fresh perspective to look at knowledge, especially brahminical knowledge, is proposed by the playwright. This provides the readers, Shobha R. suggests, an opportunity to invest their knowledge to understand how the myth is presented as a powerful tool in one's hands who intends to propagate one's ideology strongly. This technique of construction of new myths in order to subvert the domination of any exploitative knowledge is an innovation which Karnad successfully displays in his play in question.

In "The Reliable Gods and Goddesses: A Study of Androgyny, Gender Fluidity and Same-Sex Relationships," Sandhya and Kirankumar examine the concepts of sexuality, gender roles, gender fluidity and androgyny to investigate Devdutt Pattanaik's *Shikhandi: And Other Tales They Don't Tell You* to show how reliable myths and folklores are validated to sexual minorities and the society to create an all-inclusive society. Through a close analysis of few tales from the collection, Sandhya and Kirankumar assert that what is unnatural is also natural and as such the pain and suffering of the sexual minorities may be diminished. Hence, the myths on gender fluidity and same-sex relations emphasise that history may be taken into account and relearnt to affirm what was true and inclusive once.

In "Queerness in Select Stories of Devdutt Pattanaik's *Shikhandi: And Other Tales They Don't Tell You,*" Radhika focuses on the relevance of mythical stories in the present day society and their connection with queerness. Pattanaik is the first writer, she argues, who has accepted, assembled and remarked on the queer ideas in Indian mythological stories. The writer, through his retelling of myths, compares the queerness of the past to the present and touches upon individualism, patriarchy, feminism and neutrality.

R. Umamaheswari's paper "Myth and Retelling of Political Ideologies," discusses political ideologies which are recreated through the doctrines defined in the past in connection with ancient myths. She opines that myth and mythology superficially rule the political world demanding a westernised ambience in a traditional outlook. Taking cues from *No Exit, Waiting for Godot, Athava Veda,* and similar texts, she maintains that political ideologies are influenced by history and historical myths and, in a way, provide critical insights through terms such as Post-colonialism and Techno Populism.

In "*Ahalya's Awakening:* Contemporary Women through Myth," Pooja and Anuradha attempt to create responsiveness among contemporary women through the voice of Ahalya, a marginalised woman in the epic *Ramayana.* While focusing on the dilemma encountered by Ahalya in her life-long journey towards the development of her inner-self, the paper aims to foreground archetypal retelling of social, religious and philosophical aspects of contemporary society. She is a symbol of hope, Pooja and Anuradha assert, and her life suggests that self-reliance is significantly important for one' growth and face challenges of life.

Pooja Goyal deals with the recurring myth of American Dream in her paper "Retellings the Myth of American Dream and Arthur Miller's *Death of a Salesman*" and maintains that the idea of specific dream remains a myth and not a reality for Willy Loman. The concepts like economic progress and life's high standards, which are associated with American Dream, remain far-fetched ideas creating a myth of American Dream. Though it pushes him hard to achieve high economic goals, he becomes its victim and a vehicle to prove that it is all a fiasco.

In "Formation of Myths about Colonial Indian Railways: A Nineteenth Century Review," Sudipa Sardar investigates how the colonial railways got transformed into a myth and what are the sub-myths associated with it. The myth of establishing equality through railways got broken with the passage of time, especially during the partition of India.

Suneela Sharma, in her paper "Immortalising Myth through Language and Life," maintains that myths are immortalised when they become a part and parcel of our language and life. Sharma, through a brief look at various myths of east and west, argues that they have been internalised by mankind in one way or the other and, as such, have been recreated in several ways to instruct and guide. Myths and mythical characters have become the soul of our languages and cultures, and will remain, as long as we have a language to carry them along.

Tanvi Punia explores the portrayal and appropriation of the superstition of 'witches' in popular cinema in her paper "Mythology of Witchcraft and Transgressive Femininity in Mainstream Movies *The Conjuring*, *The Love Witch*, and *Bulbbul*." She investigates how it engages with the imagination of the mass audience, what idea the term 'witch' evokes in popular vocabulary, why the cult of the witch has gained such enormous popularity among the masses and in popular media, and what its popularity implies. The terms 'women' and 'power' are paradoxical in patriarchal vocabulary and the witches strongly subvert this established power structure. Tanvi also examines the third-world witches in a country like India since India, as we know, is a country full of numerous superstitions in these respects and has a rich history surrounding witches.

In "Performative, Performance and Retold Myths in Poile Sengupta's *Thus Spake Shoorpanakha, So Said Shakuni,*" Sanjeev Kumar argues that the mythical characters in question have dubious authenticity when looked at from the perspective of Performative or Performance theory. Sengupta recreates the two characters and they plead for their case in a way that attracts sympathy, at first, but toward the final scene, they become vehicles of disaster. The text and its performance, Kumar opines, are two different things and as such, provide ample evidence that the audience, the stage, the text and the actors play significant roles to put forward the intended meaning of the playwright.

The editors hope that the book will satiate the curious sensibility of the teachers and scholars, and also initiate further queries in this specific expanse of retellings of myths in contemporary times. The papers are judiciously selected to cover major filaments of the area in question. Every care has been taken to bring the book up to the anticipations of the readers, even so, the editors would be indebted to the readers for their valuable propositions and endorsements to improve the eminence of the literary contents of the book.

Editors

Works Cited

Frye, Stephen. *Mythos: The Greek Myhts Reimagined,* Chronicle Books, 2017.

Graves, Robert, editor. *New Larousse Encyclopedia of Mythology.* Hamlyn, 1968.

Kane, Kavita. "Indian Myth – The Story of Uniques Universal Value: A Conversation of Kavita Kane." Interview by Ashish Kumar Gupta, *Art and Aesthetics of Modern Mythopoeia: Literature, Myths & Revisionism,* vol II, edited by Ritushree Sengupta and Ashish K. Gupta, Vishwanatha Kaviraja Institute, 2020, pp. 340-345.

Pattanaik, Devdutt. *Indian Myhtology: Tales, Symbols, and Rituals from the Heart of the Subcontinent.* Inner Traditions, 2003.

Acknowledgements

This book is a collaborative outcome that germinated in a discussion with Dr. Ravi Bhushan, Professor and Chair in English department of BPS Mahila Vishwavidyalaya, Khanpur Kalan, Sonipat. For his contribution towards selection and conceptualisation of the theme that took hold of us and propelled us through and through, we thank him endearingly. Without the enthusiastic response of several teachers and scholars across India who thought the project worthy and submitted their papers for the book, we are in the foremost grateful as without these papers the book was not possible. We thank Prof. Ashok Verma, a colleague of Prof. Ravi Bhusan, for suggesting the title of the book and for help during selection of papers. Anyone who has done the painful task of rejecting from a lot can understand the value of sharp but fair contribution in this crucial matter. We are grateful to Dr. Himanshu Parmar, Chairperson, Department of English, Himachal Pradesh University, Shimla, for his insights and comments during the process of the editing of this anthology of papers. Dr Yash Pal, Assistant Prof. of English in the Govt. College for Women, Shahzadpur, proofread the penultimate draft and looked for glaring deviations, if any, from the latest MLA Handbook. We thank him too.

We are indebted and owe gratitude to Dr. Suresh Kumar and Ms. Rajni for their moral and familial support and for the time and energy they provided us which helped us to accomplish this task successfully. We are grateful to Arindam, Agastya, Pavishka and Daakshit – our life lines – for keeping their joy abreast and for letting us finish this task timely and, hopefully, with some degree of success, which the readers alone can judge.

We are thankful to Authorspress for materialising and shaping our concept into reality.

Anuradha

Sanjeev Kumar

Notes on Contributors

1. **Anshuman** is a Ph.D. research fellow at Indira Gandhi University, Rewari. Her area of interest includes Queer Theory, Transgender Studies, Translation and Indian Writings in English. She has contributed a number of papers in many books and research journals.
2. **Anuradha** is an Assistant Prof of English, MDSD Girls College, Ambala City. A Ph.D. from Himachal Pradesh University, Shimla, she is actively engaged in reading and writing and has edited two books – *Postmodern Voices in Contemporary Indian Writing in English* and *Postmodern Perspectives on American Literature.* She is a voracious reader and keeps on writing papers and articles for books, journals and newspapers.
3. **Kirankumar Nittali** is an Assistant Professor at the Department of English, Presidency University, Bangalore. A Ph.D. from Centre for English Studies, Central University of Jharkhand, Ranchi, he has taught English language, Communicative Skills, Business English and English literature for various courses and is having experience of over 11 years of academics in various reputed institutes. He has presented several papers at national/international conferences and published several articles and chapters in national and international journals and books.
4. **M. Samadhanam Emimal,** a Ph.D., is an Assistant Professor in the Department of English at Avinashilingam Institute of Home Science and Higher Education for Women, Coimbatore, India. She has presented several papers at national/international conferences and published several articles and chapters in national and international journals and books. Her areas of interest include Transgender Studies, Translation Cultural Studies, Comparative Studies and Diaspora.
5. **Pooja Bairagi,** a Ph.D., is an Assistant Professor of English at SMS Khalsa Labana Girls College, Barara, Ambala. She has presented a number of research papers in various national and international seminars and conferences. She has also published papers in reputed journals and books.

6. **Pooja Goyal,** a Ph.D., is an Assistant Prof of English at Govt P.G. College, Ambala Cantt. She has been serving Higher Education Department, Haryana since July 12, 2006. She has published papers in numerous journals and books. She has presented a number of research papers in various national and international seminars and conferences. Recently she has been awarded "The Super Woman Award 2022" in the category of Empowered Woman by FSI (Forever Star India) at national level for her contribution in literary, social and environmental activities.
7. **Poonam Choudhary** is an Assistant Professor of English at Harsh Vidya Mandir P.G. College, affiliated to Sri Dev Suman Uttarakhand University, Uttarakhand. She has completed her M.Phil. and Ph.D. in English from C.C.S. University, Meerut. She has successfully edited a book *Women in 21st Century Indian Literature: Contemporary Issues and Perspectives'*. Her area of interest and specialization is gender issues from diverse perspectives in Indian context. She has been awarded with young scientist award for her excellence in educational field by ARIDSS in the year 2021. Moreover, she has participated and presented papers in many seminars, workshops, and conferences and has published various papers on Indian, postcolonial and comparative literature in reputed journals and books.
8. **Radhika** is a Ph.D. research scholar in the Department of English and Foreign Languages, Central University of Haryana, Mahendergarh. She has participated and presented a number of research papers in various national and international seminars/ conferences. She has also published papers in reputed journals and books. Her areas of interest include mythology, Cultural Studies, Comparative Studies and Diaspora.
9. **Sandhya Devi N.K.** is pursuing her Ph.D. at the Department of English, Presidency University, Bengaluru. Her primary research areas are Queer Studies, Gender Studies, Cultural Studies, Partition Literature and World Literature. She has completed her MA from Jain University and has taught for 3 years in various institutions. She has published several articles and chapters in international journals and presented several papers at national/international conferences and seminars.
10. **Sanjeev Kumar** is an Assistant Prof of English at Govt P.G. College, Naraingarh, Haryana. His area of literary interest includes African American Studies, Cultural Studies, Subaltern Studies,

Performance Studies, Posthumanism and Indian Writing in English.

11. **Santosh Kumari** is an Assistant Professor of Sociology in the Department of Higher Education, Himachal Pradesh with her present posting at Govt College, Chowari, Chamba (HP). She is an alumna of JNV, Chamba and Himachal Pradesh University, Shimla. She has attended and presented numerous research papers in multiple national and international seminars and conferences. She has published several research papers in varied journals and books also.

12. **Shobha R.** is working as an Assistant Professor of English in Government First Grade College for Arts, Science and Commerce, Sira, Tumkur Dist., Karnataka. She is a creative writer and composes poems in Kannada. She has partially contributed to the translated books named *Hindutva mathu Dalitaru*, *Mahatma mathu Gurudeva Samvada*, and *Bandavala.* She has published a number of papers in various journals and books. She also writes and translates to 'Teacher' magazine in Kannada.

13. **Sudipta Sardar** is working as Vice Principal at Rabindra Bharati Mahavidyalaya. He has also taught English literature to the students of Rabindra Bharati Mahavidyala. Along with it, he has been attached as a Programme Officer of NSS in this college. He has participated in several national and international seminars. Presently, he is a Ph.D. research scholar in History Department of Calcutta University. His research focus is also colonial and postcolonial perspective in the light of history of railways and modern historical trends and historiography context.

14. **Suneela Sharma** is working as an Associate Professor of English, Govt. Degree College, Nalagarh, Distt. Solan (HP). She is a writer, actor, filmmaker, event organiser, career counsellor, yoga teacher and social worker, She completed her graduation with honours in English Literature from Panjab University, Chandigarh and thereafter Master of Arts in English Literature from Himachal Pradesh University in 1988. She did her PGCTE and PGDTE from CIEFL (now EFLU), Hyderabad and PGDDE from IGNOU. She is the first and the only Ph.D. research scholar in Himachal Pradesh in the subject of the Phonetics of English. She is the author of *The Dialectal Influences on the Spoken English in the Districts of Himachal Pradesh* which was released by Late

Honourable Chief Minister of Himachal Pradesh Shri Vir Bhadra Singh Ji on 28 January 2013.

15. **Tanvi Punia** is pursuing her Master's degree in English from Ramjas College, University of Delhi. She cleared Graduate Aptitude Test in Engineering (GATE) and qualified NET in her first attempt. She is a freelance content writer and has published articles in various newsletters, magazines and anthologies. Ms Punia has worked for various companies and start-ups around the world as a content writer and enjoys reading books, listening to podcasts, writing blogs, composing poetry, playing chess and dancing.
16. **Thejimol George** is an Assistant Professor of English at St. George's College, Aruvithura, Kerala. She has been teaching English language and literature for the last seven years. Her areas of interest include Indian Writings in English, Diaspora, Postmodern Literature, Postcolonial Literature and Trauma Studies which occupy a dominant space in the contemporary literary scenario.
17. **Umamaheswari** is an Assistant Professor in Mar Gregorios College of Arts & Science. She has also served as an English faculty as Soft Skills Trainer in various colleges. Her research interests include psychoanalysis, mythology and postmodernism.
18. **Vanya Goyal** is a Visiting Professor at Amity University, Noida. She is teaching English communication and writing skills. She has completed her M.Phil. from Amity University, and her master's degree from Sri Venkateswara College, Delhi University. She did her bachelor's from Dayalbagh University, Agra. Her areas of interest include Postcolonial Studies, Frame Narratives, and Post-modernism.
19. **Virender Pal** is an Associate Professor of English at Institute of Integrated and Honors Studies, Kurukshetra University, Kurukshetra. He has been teaching English literature and language for twenty years. He did his Ph.D. on Australian Aboriginal literature from Kurukshetra University, Kurukshetra. He has published more than forty research papers in numerous research journals and edited books. His interests include Native Literature, Indian Writing in English and Indian Literature in Translation.

20. **Yash Pal** is a B.E. in Electronics & Communication from the DCRUST, Murthal, Haryana and a Ph.D. in English from the Central Univcrsity of Himachal Pradesh, Dharamshala. He worked as Telecom Engineer in BSNL for some years and then quit to pursuc his intcrest in literature. Currently he is working in the Dept of Higher Education, Haryana as an Assistant Professor of English with his present posting at Govt College for Women, Shahzadpur, Ambala. His essay on Disaster Management won the national first prize in an open competition among all universities conducted by the Human Resource Ministry, Govt. of India. He has presented many research papers in various national and international seminars and conferences and has also contributed papers in many journals and edited books.

Contents

Chapter 1

Myths and Post-Truth: Some Conjectures on Connection

Yash Pal and Santosh Kumari

I

In a 2019 public opinion survey, the Pew Research Centre, an American think tank, reconfirmed that a significant, but reducing, number of people in America do not believe in the Darwin's theory of evolution. The idea that life on earth has evolved, and is still evolving, is a firmly established scientific theory amply corroborated by empirical evidence. Among those who accept the theory, nearly half believe it "as an instrument of God's will" (Masci). The theory had had nearly "steady" acceptors of about sixty per cent of the Americans for a long period despite the demographic variables of age, education, ideology and religious beliefs (Carroll). These findings accentuate an interesting human trait about facts and beliefs: to some of us facts do not matter. This paper tries to juxtapose this human trait regarding facts, and as a corollary regarding evidence, to social phenomena of myths and post-truth and conjectures about connection between these two phenomena.

Myths are collectively accepted narratives about characters and events, or simply stories, of usually distant past for which there is no evidence. *Oxford Advanced Learner's Dictionary* cites the word fallacy as a synonym. An individual myth is more disconcerting, vis-à-vis plausibility and possibility as perceived by modern minds as compared to when they are received in the larger mythological paraphernalia of mass belief, common rituals, festivals and religious texts. For example, in Indian context, individual feats of Hanuman, the monkey god in the great epic *Ramayana*, and in one popular instance of his powerful immovable tail in *Mahabharata*, when seen in isolation seem completely unbelievable but when ensconced in a whole Hindu mythology they seem to go well along with many more myths of many more characters.

Myths play social functions of "explanation" of facts, "justification or validation" of customs, "descriptions" of events or "healing, renewal, and inspiration" (Smith and Buxton). All these roles are laudable in themselves and seem necessary in the growth of human civilisations from primitive hunter-gathering herds to modern complex social formations. Human reason may not have progressed in leaps and bound but incrementally along with social needs and circumstances. The myths must have appeared at some point in that progress and since then some have stayed with us. Their presence in oral literatures, and in written when they were subsequently scripted, enriches our collective history. This cannot be gainsaid. However, it becomes troublesome when myths, and therefore mythologies, permeate social beliefs with mixed good and bad outcomes and are still disallowed examination for their roles. Actually myths pre-empt examination and any attempts of examination are rebuffed with a woolly but power-packed thrust of lest-you-hurt-somebody's-feelings outcry.

The rudimentary logical proposition about such a social situation in which some people are prevented from holding and disseminating views which counterweigh the so called common people's beliefs in prevailing myths may be stated in utilitarian terms like this: unless the harm caused by interrogating myths is proved to be more than by preserving their sacral forms it is counterproductive to cease the interrogation of myths. Related empirical data on harm can help here. In India, "religious gatherings and pilgrimages" are the venue, and in one strong sense, the primary cause of stampedes, which according to National Crime Records Bureau data "puts the [human] death toll . . . at 1823" from 2000 to 2012 (Illiyas et al.). Nearly all the places where these avoidable fatalities occurred are perceived and approached by devotees through the reigning myths about these places. These myths as stories are interesting qua stories. But in light of the above fact of traffic and occasional fatal flare-ups myths give rise to the question as to why such and such fellows, including children, women, and men, lost their lives. Any fellow human being should shudder at such a death and more so when one happens to be a witness to a pilgrim death by such accidents as above. Do people, who witnessed others succumb, breathe easy that they were lucky or do they just wade through the gamble that is life? Nevertheless pilgrimage seems to be increasing in the world led by all sorts of advertisement and subsidising. No doubt that such tragedies cause the governments to act towards improving towards reduction of such tragedies. This refers back us to the question of the utilitarian weighing of examining myths for their good and bad outcomes.

Smith and Buxton write: "As with all religious symbolism, there is no attempt to justify mythic narratives or even to render them plausible. Every myth presents itself as an authoritative, factual account, no matter how much the narrated events are at variance with natural law or ordinary experience." It may be said that at a given time in a given culture myths are so inviolably preserved and protected that they seem necessary for that culture's identity. This raises the questions of who has a say in identifying a culture, who or what is kept hidden, who controls it and to what extent and finally who benefits through cultural capital. It is usually anathema to raise such questions because they make way for rather tedious, embattled and empirically contesting answers and pseudo-answers. Before such an attempt it is perhaps apt to justify why myths exist.

II

Neither empirically, that is to the senses and the measurable, nor theoretically world can be static but it can be so in abstractions, howsoever complex. It is possible only in movement. But one can picture and perceive the world at a moment and milieu. At a given moment world needs picturing and from what vantage point it is perceived becomes of utmost importance. If minor facts about details are allowed to dissolve for a moment then we can have one picture such as this: the planet earth is a habitat to roughly 8 billion people who speak thousands of languages in spread out regions of varied climatic and geographic conditions divided in nearing 200 countries[i] and all these countries are at various junctures or stages of 'development' which encapsulates average life conditions of peoples of these countries, wherein there is usually great diversity and disparity. Rich and poor, sick and hearty, secure and precarious, empowered or disempowered, mover or moved, challenger and challenged, lettered and unlettered, identified and unmarked – all these contingent propositions of binaries as the end points of the spectrums and many more flow in and out of each other to create the great and dizzying flux of the world that we can picture. Obviously, there can be many more pictures of the world. Any real picture of the world taken at a time is bound with experiential reality. When the experiential reality of all living creatures is summed up, adding other living beings than humans, the perceiving mind fails to grasp and turns towards simplification, fictionalisation, mythologizing, falsification and factionalisation. Stepping back, so to say, one can consider a child perceiving the world through family, school, friends and community. This perception grows, though not necessarily, as a person grows and eventually becomes complex in myriad and unfathomable ways. It becomes *virat*, which means immense in Sanskrit. So the summed up reality and the *virat*ness or the immensity of it beg and justify these processes of simplification etc. and thus render the world ideologically to us. Ideological in the basic sense here means any set of ideas that sustains individuals or groups. Scientific method enumerates, classifies, organises and criticizes and that too in a disinterested and methodical way to understand natural and social world. This method, by far, remains the real and robust way to apprehend reality. Now it is possible to aver that science and scientific method fail to touch both the primitive world of myths and contemporary world of post-truth.

III

Myths are requisite handles for the infinite, moving, material reality of the world and they may have begun well but are not aging that well because they seem to act as stoppages towards true and realistic outlook towards the world and its problems. We can take a factually established problem like climate change and examine how myths and religiosity imbued in them preclude not only the true understanding of such problems but also prevent their solutions. But before that we can go to the root of the word myth and its history to problematise the justifications and functions attributed to myths. In this respect the beginning part of the entry on myth in the *Macmillan Dictionary of Religion* must be quoted at length:

> [Myth was] Originally a Greek word, with the simple meaning of 'a story'. For Christian apologists and many enlightenment thinkers, a myth was a story believed by some to be true, but known in fact to be false. 'Myth' was thus contrasted with 'revelation' for Christians and 'history' for philosophers. These senses of the term still circulate, and are used when certain features of a story are singled out for emphasis, e.g. a lack of historicity. But students of religion and culture have tended to adopt the sense of myth developed by the romantic movement: myth is thus an 'important' story, or a derivative of an important story. Thanks to the

romantics, the emphasis is shifted from the story in itself to the way it is regarded. ("myth")

It is clear in at least two ways that myth and their collective current dominant stature, rather than true worth, is neither natural nor irreversible. The first is the historic accident of the romantic movement as related in the above quote and the second is the fact that some myths are relegated to historical curiosities while others thrive. To put it slightly differently with an inclusion of element of human agency and inversion of perspective it can be said that certain people thrive with the help of perpetuation of myths, their regarded value and concurrent elision of the fact of their falsehood. One prominent example of the latter is the unofficial suppression of *The Hindus: An Alternative History* by Wendy Doniger. The reason for the suppression by one Indophile is that the book's readers get "a history of India as seen largely through the eyes of people on the margins of life – ... women, low castes, tribals, and Dalits" and many other "mostly dissident tones," "creative gestures", and "especially those that generated significant social protest and religious change" (Shulman). Cultural and religious elitism is at work in the processes here. In case of India, then, one can surmise that myths too are controlled by the caste and class elites and certain myths are propagated unabated and their prevalence is then used to justify several roles that myths play that sociologists or religious scholars corroborate. In case of other myths that can unseat totally, or partially unsettle the meanings of, dominant myths it is possible to say that their quality is contrarian as mentioned above i.e., of protest and change. Now it is possible to view the definitional thrust of myth as stories that are neither amenable nor inviting the scrutiny of scientific method. Rather annoyed and violent social and legal sanctions work in the disguised manner of sanctimonious religiosity to guard the myths and mythologies in their position of power.

IV

In 2016 the Oxford Dictionaries selected 'post-truth' as the "international word of the year" and defined it as an adjective that means a situation in which "objective facts are less influential in shaping public opinion than appeals to emotion and personal belief" (Flood). While describing the word, the Oxford University Press website illustrates the word with a glaring example of usage through the Twitter handle of The Economist magazine. The message says:

"Obama founded ISIS. George Bush was behind 9/11. Welcome to post-truth politics" ("Word of the Year 2016"). The idea of post-truth and consequent post-truth politics has generated a sizable literature. In its Essential Knowledge Series, MIT Press published *Post-Truth* by Lee McIntyre in 2018 and the book captures various strands of the history and progression of the idea. After an attempt at the definition of the term, McIntyre starts with charting the roots of post-truth in science-denialism, which he connects with the right-wing ideology and finally but partially implicates postmodernism, which is loosely connected with the left-wing academics. While trying to define it, McIntyre quotes a conversation that typifies the post-truth situation in which a factually verified data about the murder rate in America is discussed on camera. The then president of the USA, Donald Trump, also lied about the same fact to spread paranoia and fear to garner votes or allegiance. The conversation between a CNN reporter Alisyn Camerota and a Trump stand-in Newt Gingrich goes like this:

CAMEROTA: Violent crime is down. The economy is ticking up.

GINGRICH: It is not down in the biggest cities.

CAMEROTA: Violent crime, murder rate is down. It is down.

GINGRICH: Then how come it's up in Chicago and up in Baltimore and up in Washington?

CAMEROTA: There are pockets where certainly we are not tackling murder.

GINGRICH" Your national capital, your third biggest city –

CAMEROTA: But violent crime across the country is down.

GINGRICH: The average American, I will bet you this morning, does not think crime is down, does not think we are safer.

CAMEROTA: But it is. We are safer and it is down.

GINGRICH: No, that's just your view.

CAMEROTA: It's a fact. These are the national FBI facts.

GINGRICH: But what I said is also a fact. … The current view is that liberals have a whole set of statistics that theoretically may be right, but it's not where human beings are.

CAMEROTA: But what you're saying is, but hold on Mr. Speaker because you're saying liberals use these numbers, they use this sort of magic math. These are the FBI statistics. They're not a liberal organisation. They're a crime-fighting organisation.

GINGRICH: No, but what I said is equally true. People feel more threatened.

CAMEROTA: Feel it, yes. They feel it, but the facts don't support it.

GINGRICH: As a political candidate, I'll go with how people feel and let you go with the theoreticians. (McIntyre 3-4)

It is clear from the above conversation how post-truth is different from plain lies. The aspect of feeling makes it different. This aspect of feeling is also a factor in myths that prevail in a culture. The denial of science or scientific method is also common to both myths and post truth. In fact, McIntyre has called this aspect of science-denial necessary "Road Map for Understanding Post-Truth" as he devotes a whole chapter of the book on this. And in 2021, he takes this aspect of science denial and apparently found it so pivotal to the contemporary culture of hyper-connectedness and disinformation that he wrote a book on it. Anyone aware of the mass media and its content circulating in silos can attest to a lot of bunkum in it and this has to do a lot with low penetration of education and scientific attitude. The highfalutin regard for truth being a rule than exception, however only a few have a method to reach truth. All kinds of biases and crutches come to take place of serious systematic search for truth particularly in societies reaching after mass literacy, and thereafter, towards mass education. To take a recent example, at the raging peak of raging Covid-19 in India all kinds of herbal remedies were rife amongst people and even official sanction for such remedies was just about announced. In India, the plurality of possible types of lives is still staggering and for any observer only statistics and data seem to provide a dependable resort. Myths in India are treated to an altogether different level. Kumbh Mela might illustrate the currency of myths as it draws perhaps the largest crowd in the world. In 2019 the number of pilgrims who visited Kumbh crossed 240 million (John). And the myths around the place called Praygraj, one from the four such, where the Kumbh took place in 2019, is that here the "drops of the essence of immortality were spilled from an urn being fought over by gods and demons" (Safi). By bathing at the confluence of the rivers people get cleanse of their past sins, such is the lore.

V

Finally, the following conjectures are made here in regard to connection between post-truth phenomenon and the prevalence of myths. Both myths and post-truth are antithetical to the common human reason but find home in their story-telling, narrative-generating aspect. Understood this way, they also stand against the science, scientific method, critical thinking and moral progress. While myths tend to perpetuate inherited inequalities via keeping the world deity-laced and magic-bound, post-truth impedes the scientific and democratising impulses that harbinger moral progress by keeping us foolish about the realities that eventually catch up with us in small, medium, and large scale phenomena. Both myths and post-truth, as phenomena, partake in the discourses that shape the public policies usually towards worse than better. For example, in India, the quantum of religious tourism and many other associated rituals, when seen from the perspective of endemic poverty, raise important question of priorities within poor families of allocation of available funds to such aspects of life as education and nutrition. Though the research on the ideological leanings of these two phenomena is inadequate, the conjecture is that for the right-leaning to dominate in creation or perpetuation of both myths and post-truth.

Countries or nation states are not the only way to overview the world in this way. There could be others such as according to continents, linguistic and cultural cohorts etc.

Works Cited

Carroll, Sean B. "Is America Evolving on Evolution?" *Scientificamerican.com*. 11 Feb. 2014. https://www.scientificamerican.com/article/is-america-evolving-on-evolution.

Flood, Alison. "Post-truth Named Word of the Year by Oxford Dictionaries." *Guardian*. 15 Nov. 2016. www.theguardian.com/books/2016/nov/15/post-truth-named-word-of-the-year-by-oxford-dictionaries.

Illiyas, Faisel T., et al. "Human Stampedes during Religious Festivals: A Comparative Review of Mass Gathering Emergencies in India." *International Journal of Disaster Risk Reduction*, vol. 5, Sept. 2013, pp. 10-18. Elsevier, doi.org: 10.1016/j.ijdrr.2013.09.003.

John, Kenneth. "A Record over 24 Crore People Visited Kumbh-2019, More Than Total Tourists in UP in 2014-17." *Hindustan Times*. 21 May 2019.

McIntyre, Lee C. *Post-Truth*. MIT P, 2018.

Masci, Davi. "Darwin in America: Evolution Debates in the United States". *Pewresearch.org*. 6 Feb. 2019. www.pewresearch.org/religion/2019/02/06/darwin-in-america-2.

"myth". Michael Pye, editor. *Macmillan Dictionary of Religion*. Macmillan P, 1994, pp. 175-76.

Safi, Michael. "Kumbh Mela: Hindus Converge for Largest-Ever Human Gathering". *Guardian*. 15 Jan. 2019.

Shulman, David. "A Passion for Hindu Myths." Rev. of the *Hindus: An Alternative History* by Wendy Doniger. *New York Review of Books*, 19 Nov. 2009.

Smith, Jonathan Z, and Richard G. A. Buxton. "myth". *Encyclopædia Britannica*. Encyclopaedia Britannica Ultimate Reference Suite. Encyclopædia Britannica, 2010.

"Word of the Year 2016." *Oxford Languages*. 2016. www.languages.oup.com/word-of-the-year/2016/.

Chapter 2

Disney Animated Adaptations as Modern Mythology and Folklore

Vanya Goyal

In ancient times, when scientific learning was limited, myths and folklores were created by people to explain the origins of the world around them. Over time, these tales became a part of cultural memory shaping many traditions and practices of different cultures around the world. Christopher Booker explains in his book *The Seven Basic Plots: Why We Tell Stories* how, "one of the deepest human needs for an explanation and description of how the world began was met by our ability to imagine and create stories about it. There is no culture in the world which does not possess at least one great story to account for how the world came into being" (544). Jack Zipes, in his book *Happily Ever After: Fairy Tales, Children and Cultural Industry*, maintains that the storytellers of those times, who were creative in the art of story-telling were revered members of the society as most people were not articulate and these storytellers served a very important function of transmitting age-old myths and fairy tales and helping people remember and retain cultural memory (63).

In late 1890s, early filmmakers like Geoges Méliès began experimenting with motifs of fairy tales and folklores like the story of Cinderella. The genre of film was an ideal medium to articulate these age-old fairy tales and myths since magic could be shown more easily and more wonderfully than in theatre. But lack of sound in films during that time meant that the stories had to be simplified and turned into a purely visual experience rather than an oral one (67).

By the time Walt Disney started making movies during the 1930s, sound and colour had already been introduced as the medium of film. He and his brother started in early 1920a by creating Micky Mouse cartoons and short films like *Puss in the Boots* (1922) and *Little Red Riding Hood* (1922). In 1934 though, Disney finally became ready to produce a film on his own and instead of writing a new story chose to focus on the age-old fairy tale of *Snow White and the Seven Dwarfs* (1812), first formally published by German storyteller duo, the Brothers Grimm. After three years, Disney released its animated movie, *Snow White and the Seven Dwarfs* (1937). "It was the first animated film in history", argues Zipes, which was based on a fairy tale and was made with colour and music" (89).

The movie was a resounding critical and box-office success making international earnings of more than $8 million during its initial release, thus cementing Disney animation as the number one filmmaker based on myths and fairy tales. It set a precedent for many of the subsequent Disney Productions (Kaufman, 158). Disney's formula of taking a well-known fairy tale or folklore and beautifying characters while editing the story more suited to get the desired happy ending became Disney's success mantra in the coming years.

The 1950 *Cinderella* animation feature, again based on the tale published by The Brothers Grimm marked a turning point for Disney animation studio financially as it earned more money on its initial release than *Snow White and the Seven Dwarfs* (Ohmer 232). Since then, Disney has been using the modern technology of animation to effectively and more creatively tell ancient mythical stories and fairy tales which mostly come from oral tradition with long and rich cultural history.

Since the successful release of *Snow White and the Seven Dwarfs*, Disney has grown from a film studio to a multinational-media conglomerate – a cultural force that has made itself almost synonymous with contemporary understandings and experiences of childhood. The studio subsequently created many more stories based on different myths and folklores which ultimately reinforced the American way of life. Even today, Disney remains a dominant and influential player in the market of children entertainment business all round the world (Wasko 27). According to Schweizer, around 74 percent of children have the urge to copy what they have seen in movies (Schweizer 199). This means that children mostly accept the animated stories of Disney as the truth and do not question the representativeness of the shown culture. Children identify themselves with characters in movies and this can influence their perception of cultures in the world.

As Zipes puts it, Disney is in the "Culture Industry" (155). So, naturally, if stories are shipped around the world to different cultures as commercial products, they will be required to change as the industry demands. To this end, Disney is known to make a few tweaks in the original plot of the stories and cultures that these stories are set in. This phenomenon has been dubbed as 'Disneyfication', first coined by Peter K Fallon. 'Disneyfication', refers to transformation of a cultural folklore or historical story by stripping away the original material of its character and then beautifying as well as sanitising it to make it more simplified and beautiful so that it adheres to a sense of American uniformity and is fit for mass consumption.

In the Disney version, all characters are made "cuter and more beautiful" to fit mass sensibilities and creative license is taken upon in order to edit the stories and help the main characters get their desired happy ending much more suited for mass consumption (Wasko 21).

The example of this can be seen in the stories of *The Little Mermaid* and *Tangled* which are structurally quite different from their source material even as the main story line remains the same. This hybridisation becomes even more apparent when the stories are taken from other cultures. In meeting the demands of diverse global audience coming from a variety of cultural origins and because there has been a recent boost in the demand for cultural productions, Disney Animation Studios, which caters to this global audience, plays an important role by influencing their audience's interpretation of other cultures. This is especially true for their young audience that is much more impressionable and much less likely to question the appropriateness of representation.

The study looks at three folklores taken from three different sources and how the Disney Animation Studios turned these classic stories into a disneyfied version which have become global favourites of children and adults alike, even as they have been stripped of many of their original traits. The study will focus on the tales of *Hercules, Mulan* and *Moana.* The study will use a comparative approach to see the similarities and distinctions between the original stories and their Disney versions to see how Disney Animation Studios revised these stories, their characters and even the settings in order to make them more fit for their target audience.

Hercules, released in 1997, marked Disney's second attempt at portraying the mythology of ancient Greece after *Fantasia* (1940). It is based on the tales of celebrated ancient Greek hero Heracles (Latin- Hercules). In this modern retelling, Disney sought to give a brief glimpse of ancient Greek mythology and the many Gods inhabiting the mythical space but edited it to become more suitable for its young American (and global) audience. While the animation used the latinised version of Heracles' name, the other gods kept their original Greek names. Since the movies were targeted towards a young audience, the story was sanitised to become more appropriate for their consumption. This meant that all mentions of extramarital, incestuous and sexual relationships were omitted. Thus, in the Disney version, instead of being the half mortal son of Zeus and Alcmene, Hercules was turned into the son of Zeus and his wife Hera, the queen of gods and goddesses, who was adopted by Alcmene and Amphitrion. Thus, Hera's jealousy is removed from the equation and instead Hades, the god of the underworld, is made into the villain of the story. Hades is shown as a jealous god who envys Zeus' position and wants to rule Mount Olympus. He sends his minions to murder Hercules, who is fated to stop Hades from ruling Mount Olympus. As a result of the minions failed attempt, Hercules still grows up on earth as a half-human half-god figure but remains unaware of his true parents unlike the original Heracles.

This modern retelling of Hercules is depicted with Christian undertones as we can see when Hades and Zeus are pitted against each other in a show of good versus evil when, in original myth, Hades is never shown to be jealous of Zeus. Hercules is shown as a man who must overcome his obstacles in order to complete his heroic journey (Campbell 94). Even the underworld portrayed in Disney's *Hercules*, looks more like a Christian hell than a Greek underworld (March 341). While there is no distinction of heaven and hell in Disney's version of underworld, it is still depicted in sombre tones with Hades a demonic figure. This is completely different from the ancient Greek understanding of life after death. Death was a natural and inevitable part in ancient Greek culture and they never perceived Hades as an evil or satanic figure. Even the muses that act as a chorus in the movie possess definite Christian undertones as they sing the "Gospel of Truth".

There are various other distinctions like the absence of Heracles' twin half-brother Iphicles and even Hercules' doubt in his own abilities as the original Heracles of the ancient Greek myths is never shown to doubt himself or his abilities. The story follows the typical Disney formula of a hero/heroine who has something to prove and who finds a 'magical/supernatural aid' that helps them along their journey and fulfil their true purpose. In *Hercules*, this magical aid comes in the form of Zeus himself, Hercules flying horse Pegasus and many other supernatural creatures of Heracles' *Twelve Labours*. Although Hercules' heroic feats are shown much like in the original tale, the final message of the movie is quite different from ancient Greek sensibilities. While ancient Greeks valued glory and bravery above all, as can be seen in the stories of Heracles, Achilles and Persues, Disney showcases the value of strength of heart over physical strength. Disney's Hercules turns down glory and immortality in the favour of his mortal love.

In this sense, Hercules, like many of other Disney protagonists, fulfils the adventure journey illustrated by Campbell. Campbell's hero receives a "call for adventure", gets supernatural aid, then pass on the first threshold only to be swallowed and then get reborn (literally or metaphorically). Then he is tested again and gets a boon after becoming triumphant. In the end, the hero either returns to share their wisdom or remains forever in the blessed Eutopia.

This same journey is undertaken by many other Disney protagonists including Mulan in Disney's 1998 animated film *Mulan*. The story of *Mulan* was borrowed from Chinese Folktale of Hua Mulan (*The Ballad of Mulan*). The original story of the Ballad of Mulan, believed to be composed between 4th and 6th century in China tells the story of a dutiful young daughter who is forced to impersonate as a male in order to take the place of her aging father who was commissioned to serve in the Chinese military. It remained an oral ballad for a long time until it was compiled in an anthology of lyrics titled *Yuefu Shiji* (Poems from Yuefu), by a scholar named Guo Maoqian. The ballad comprised of only 392 characters, telling a story of Hua Mulan who takes the place of her elderly father to join the war during the reign of the Northern Dynasty (386-581 AD) at the orders of the Khan ruler that one male representative from each family must join the army to defend against invaders. As her father was too aged to face the atrocities of the war and she had no brother, Mulan decided to replace her father by disguising herself as a male. After fighting in the war and becoming victorious, Mulan revealed her true identity to the shock of her comrades.

The idea of filial duty is paramount to the story of the original folktale. The Mulan of the original tale is portrayed as a young and gentle household icon who epitomizes filial piety and loyalty towards her nation and whose true identity is only revealed after the war is over. On the other hand, Disney's Mulan is depicted as tomboyish figure who is pronounced unsuitable for marriage and sets out to the war in order to prove her worth to the society and to her parents. Thus, even as the basic premise of Mulan impersonating a male to go to the war remains more or less the same, the motivation of the character undergoes a massive change, ultimately shifting the focus of the story. This change of character from a gentle, dutiful Mulan to a tomboyish, rebellious Mulan set on proving her worth was done in accordance with the third wave feminist idea of a coveted independent woman who was capable of achieving everything a man can achieve (Setiawati 95). In this sense, the character of *Mulan* is Americanized into a story about a young independent woman, in order be more fit for the consumption of young American audience. We see this Americanisation in Mulan's tomboyish character and her American accent. She even enjoys breakfast of sausages and fried eggs. Along with this, Mushu, Mulan's dragon, side-kicks (voiced by Eddie Murphy) in American accent full of American street-smart slangs. Even the ancestral spirits can be seen dancing to westernised music, a stark deviation from the original tale (Chan, Tian, Xiong, 117).

It can be seen in the making of Mulan how Disney adapts tales from across various cultures and then makes them more American or 'Disneyfies' to reflect the American ideal. By portraying Mulan as a feminist icon seeking independence, Disney also raises questions about gender that were not a part of the original Ballad of Mulan. In the Disney version, Mulan's motivation for going to the war is to prove her worth to her family and the society after the matchmaker deems her a disgrace to her family. This is in opposition to the original story where the original Mulan is shown as a household icon who only impersonates a male because she cares for her father and wants to fulfil her duty towards her nation.

Disney's *Mulan* became a feminist icon for many young girls who saw themselves in the adventurous, clumsy and tomboyish Mulan. The character of Mulan presented a new age feminist icon, much different from the earlier female Disney characters who followed the perfect daughter stereotype, possessing patience, beauty and grace. The movie was a huge global success, grossing over $304 million even though it got mixed reception in China itself. As Tian and Xiong point out, this led to a Disneyfication of Mulan, turning her from the gentle, dutiful daughter from the original Ballad of Mulan to a modern age feminist icon – rebellious and adventurous in nature (Tian and Xiong 122). Disney's Mulan is more adventurous and headstrong as compared to the gentle, obedient female ideal. This is the reason she is rejected by the matchmaker who deems her a disgrace to her family. This not only brings shame to her family but also hurts Mulan's self-esteem. Thus, in the Disney movie, Mulan sets out to war, disguised as a man just like in the original tale but she has an additional motivation of proving her worth to herself and to the society. Even as the original plot remains the same, with Mulan impersonating a man to replace her father, emerging victorious in the war and returning to her household duty instead of accepting the royal reward, Mulan of the Disney movie, is inherently different from the original folklore. The animated version of Mulan sends a message about self-affirmation and belief in oneself as opposed to the moral of filial piety and national loyalty advocated by the original story.

Many other cultural aspects of the original story were also changed which can be seen when the emperor bows down to Mulan in praise of her brave deeds and Mulan even hugs him. This would never happen in reality as the emperor bowing down to any civilian would be considered disgraceful. The addition of Mushu, the red dragon, Mulan's meeting and subsequent rejection by the matchmaker as well as her revelation and dismissal from the army and praise from the emperor are some of the key distinctions made by the studio. The setting is also different as the original Mulan was set during the reign of Northern Dynasty while the animation is set during the rule of the Hans. The makeup and traditions showcased in the animation are also borrowed from a variety of periods and parts of China. In this way, even as the original plot of the story remains the same, the change in the motivation of the character and also in various cultural nuances make *Mulan* considerably different from its source material.

We see a similar altercation in the story of *Moana* (2016). Set in the Polynesian island of Motunui, Moana tells the story about the headstrong daughter of the village chief, who is chosen by the ocean to restore the lost relic with the ancient goddess Te Fiti. In the story, Moana must fulfil her destiny and find the legendary demigod Maui so as to restore the relic and save her island from the blight. Although the plot of the story is original, the writers drew inspiration from a multitude of Polynesian myths. In the movie, Disney took care to highlight the Polynesian culture through the story, its characters and other small details. According to the representatives from Disney, this tale is Disney's attempt at creating an explanation for a mysterious event in Polynesian history which is known as the 'Long Pause' wherein the Polynesians stopped voyaging for almost 2000 years.

The beginning of the story illustrates how the celebrated Goddess Te Fiti and giver of life who used a pounamu stone as a source of her power (her heart) had it stolen from her by the shapeshifting demi-god Maui. Following an attack by the volcanic monster, Te Kā, Maui loses his powers and his magical fish hook and the inhabitants of the island are prevented from voyaging over the sea for over a millennium. Disney borrowed from various Polynesian cultures and also featured their celebrated demi-god figure Maui that appears in many of the Polynesian folklores. In the movie, Maui is presented as a heavily masculine figure with a body full of tattoos and who is quite obese in appearance. This was heavily criticized by the Polynesian audience some of whom complained about the appearance of their celebrated demi-god who has a thin appearance with a face of a boy on the verge of adolescence.

Maui's hypermasculinity and his self-confident personality is a perfect representation of the strong American masculinity. Even though the story is based in Polynesia, the characters "feel American" as we can see when Maui, voiced by Dwayne 'Rock' Johnson, uses American gestures and lingo (Streiff and Dundes 131). According to Dundes, Maui's fish hook represents his hypermasculinity. In the story, Mau is shown as a mixture of the collective Polynesian folklore from different parts of the culture. He is also given a backstory where he was abandoned by his parents into the ocean and made into a demigod because the gods took pity on him. A sympathetic back story is a typical feature of the Disney movies where in mischievous and even villainous characters are given a sympathetic background so as the audience can not only understand their motivation but also forgive some of their darker actions. In this way, the well-known Polynesian figure is edited in order to fit the Disney formula.

The figures of Te Fiti and Te Kā who are shown to be the same entity in the movie is actually a combination of two distinct Polynesian mythical gods. The fertile and life-giving Te Fiti, who is arguably based on a variety of goddesses named Hina, is set in contrast with the monstrous and demonic Te Kā which is also in accordance with Disney's good versus evil philosophy. Te Kā, the volcanic demon with a large, monsterous body could be based on the

Hawaiian Godddess of Volcanoes called Pele, who is infamous for her temper and her jealous nature. In this way, Disney gives a magical twist to the Polynesian historical period of the 'Long Pause', incorporating a variety of Polynesian mythological figures. The story, although set in the real island of Motinui, is shown as a hybrid of many Polynesian cultures. During the song sequence of "Where you are", we see a variety of Polynesian attires and ways of greeting ranging from Hawaai, to New Zealand and Maori. Although the movie portrays Polynesian culture and its mythology in great detail, Disney was criticized for using the coconuts which is also a Polynesian slang and the Plumeria flower which only came to Hawaii after their interaction with the European culture.

In conclusion, it can be said that Disney Animation Studios played an important role by popularising ancient myths and folklores by using the modern medium of animation especially with regards to its young audience. This puts the movie-making conglomerate in a very powerful position and by changing and editing parts of original myths and folk tales, Disney not only creates a more Americanised version of these tales but also shapes and alters the perceptions of various cultures and ancient myths in the minds of its young audience. The Disney formula of sanitising and beautifying a story to make it more fit for mass consumption is a double-edged sword. While it successfully popularises these modern versions of age-old myths, it also deeply (sometimes even negatively) impacts our understanding of other cultures.

Works Cited

Booker, C.*The Seven Basic Plots: Why We Tell Stories.* Continuum, 2011.

Cempbell, J. *The Hero with a Thousand Faces. Abacus.* 2008.

Hercules. Directed by Ron Clements and John Musker. Disney, 1997.

Kaufman, J. B. *Before Snow White.* Film History, 1993.

March, J. *Cassell's Dictionary of Classical Mythology.* Cassell & Co. 2001.

Mulan. Directed by R. Hsiao and C. Sanders, Walt Disney Pictures, 1998.

Moana. Directed by Ron Clements and John Musker. Walt Disney Pictures, 2016.

Ohmer, S. "'That Rags to Riches Stuff': Disney's Cinderella and the Cultural Space of Animation'. *Film History*, 1993.

Setiawati, B. "Americanisation of Non-American Stories in Disney Films". 20 Dec. 2021, http://dx.doi.org/10.18326/rgt.v1i1.81-114.

Streiff, M., and Dundes, L. 'From Shapeshifter to Lava Monster: Gender Stereotypes in Disney's *Moana.*' Film History, 2017.

Tian, C., and Xiong, C. "A Cultural Analysis of Disney's *Mulan* with Respect to Translation." 2013.

Wasko, J. *Understanding Disney.* Polity Press, 2001.

Zipes, J. *Happily Ever After: Fairy Tales, Children, and the Culture Industry.* Routledge. 1997.

---."Breaking the Disney Spell." in *The Classic Fairy Tales*, edited by M. Tatar. Norton & Co., 1999.

Chapter 3

Eliciting Truth and Social Reality: A Postmodern Critique on Retold Fairytales

M. Samadhanam Emimal

Fairytale scripts life and becomes an integral part of our lives and existence. Through its narrative embellishments and felicitous enchantment of simple form and human-specific themes, fairytales cut deep into our conscious and shapes our imaginative potential. The internalised pattern of the fairytale sculpts our instinctual behaviour and exerts an influential perspective towards life and other crucial function concerning human society. The traditional tales impart restrictive knowledge, abstracted from dominant ideologies that control human assimilation of culture and socialisation. Through its entrenched patterns and its underlying ideology, the classical fairytales manipulate our understanding.

As a dominant cultural narrative, the traditional fairytales became an indispensable political conduit that controlled every aspect of society. The traditional fairytale genre through its structured pattern, genre marker, functional trope and narrative features, imparts a conservative perspective towards cultural knowledge, gender formulation, social paradigm and other crucial facets of human life and society. Because of its metanarrative status, the constrictive knowledge imparted through the traditional fairytale becomes the popular imaginative formality and presumptive thinking trend. Through its metanarrative authority and adhesive hegemonic interest, classical tales establish its slant ideology, ingrained principles and conventional idealisation as standard formulations that limit genre's evolvement and human comprehension.

Postmodernism dawned as a reaction against this encompassing and utopian silhouette of the classical fairytale. Postmodernism, through its creative tenet, simplifies the concept of truth, reason and reality behind every formulaic pattern dictated by the metanarrative tales on the empirical ground. Postmodernism denaturalises and deconstructs the grandnarrative stance of the classical fairytale by exposing its manipulative strategies. The classical tales that seemed as innocent tales are no longer inculpable narratives rather a textual artifice that executed the intended actions of the bourgeois class. The concept of absolute truth presented in classical fairytales is distorted by postmodernism. The grandnarratives that seemed to exhibit objective truth is no longer a factual entity rather a fabricated strategy intended to impose certain patterned notion that favour their cause. The classical fairytales narrative through its narrative felicity emphasises the significance of truth claim, by making it appear more natural and familiar entity without any dissimulating appearance. But, postmodernism through its narrative strategies unmask the camouflaged depiction and exposes its fabricated method in instilling the so-called absolute truth.

The grandnarratives inveterate the concept of truth as an abstract entity, that is beyond questioning. The mininarratives through their innovative textual formulation alter this conception of truth. According to postmodern ideology, truth is not an objective articulation of factuality rather a 'social construct' with a subjective agreement. In this regard, Standley J. Grenz aptly comments saying, "There is no absolute truth, rather truth is relative to the community in which we participate" (8). The so-called absolute truth is not a neutral standpoint rather dependent social interlace between a subjective judgment and societal value.

The metanarratives are not framed based on the logical empirical ground but on the grounds of accepted stories that favour their determinate factor. According to one of the postmodern critics Richard Rorty, truth is nothing but an "inter subjective agreement or solidarity" (13) incorporated with principles of rationality and hierarchy. He also says that the "notion of accurate representation is simply an automatic and empty compliment which we pay to those beliefs which are successful in helping us to do what we want to do" (*Philosophy* 10). For instance, in classical fairytales men being valiant saviours and women being domesticated is not a natural systemic tradition rather a constructed agreement that favours the bourgeois class, the dominant force of the society. This concept of women being domesticated and possessing the attributes of patience, passivity, self-sacrifice and immanent submission is not an inherent trait. It is rather a social construction inveterated by a patriarchal society, naturalised through various ineludible customs and ritualised practices. The classical tale's portrayal of "female character, encoded with the ideological positioning of women are accordingly passive, objectified, positioned as prize or reward for consumption by an active aggressive male subject" (Cranny-Francis 87) is entitled and is imposed on the society as a natural entity. The naturalisation process is carried over by both oral and literary tales. These narratives strongly convinced that these customs and beliefs are natural and are of absolute significance. Presumptively, they are made into absolute truth that cannot be questioned or denied.

The metanarratives appropriated the concept of absolute truth based on intersubjective agreement and solidarity. Rorty, in his book *Truth and Progress*, points out two major ways in which narrative appropriation takes place: first, "by telling the story of their contribution to the society," and the second, "to describe themselves as standing in immediate relation to a non-human reality" (21). Similarly, the classical tales also established the bourgeois ideals as standardised custom and absolute truth through their narratives. The classical tales through their narrative efficiency erased the distinction between the natural and socially manipulated ideas. The stories narrated, incognisantly convinced the community to accept and to internalise it as a natural custom. The truth claim or objective truth advocated in the stories or, in the particular fairytale is a transcultural sort of rationality that cannot be denied, thus, became an absolute truth. The intersubjective agreement exhibited through the narratives suffices their [Bourgeois] demanded intentions in a contestable manner. The concept of truth is rewoven to accommodate the standards of one particular hegemonic power and transubstantiated them into an inviolable entity.

The intersubjective agreement or solidarity grounded on so-called objectivity, Rorty argues, exhibits the concept of truth as an "expression of an ahistorical human nature" (*Truth* 22) making it a common phenomenon with universal appeal. For instance, the trope of the wicked stepmother, used in classical tales like "Cinderella," "Snow White," "Hanzel and Gretel", etc. is portrayed as a natural human behaviour in an evasive manner. Irrespective of any differences, the trope of the wicked stepmother is never altered and made into a universal accepted stereotype. This concept of the step mother being wicked is made more comfortable and natural, instead of accepting the fact that mothers with cruel hearts who treat their children unfairly do exist in society. In this regard, Rorty aptly comments saying, "There is nothing to be said about truth, save that each of us will commend as true those beliefs which he or she finds good to believe" (*Objectivity* 24).

The concept of truth is not an independent, abstract concept rather a constructed one, to exercise power politics. The idea of 'what is truth?' is decided by the dominant hegemonic force that confronts every course of action by dictating and governing its operating schema. Metanarrative is one such elucidative tool used by bourgeois to exercise their power. The fabricated idea of truth finds its full expression with natural ease in metanarratives. Postmodernism, on the other hand, distorts this idea of metanarrative through mininarrative and its creative formulation. The mininarratives do not seek to totalise rather they demure the classicity of the metanarrative by exposing its deceptive nature.

Postmodernism exposes the artificial constructedness and manoeuvring ways through which metanarratives feigned their naturalness. As Linda Hutcheon points outs, postmodernism's initial concern is to, "de-naturalise some of the dominant features of our way of life; to point out that those entities that we unthinkingly experience as "natural" are in fact "cultural" made by us" (2). The conservatism of the traditional and established truth delineated through metanarratives has undergone an abrupt transformation in mininarratives. This alters the very disposition of truth and its significance. Postmodernism through mininarratives challenge "our mimetic assumptions about representation: assumptions about its transparency and common-sense naturalness" (Hutcheon, 32).

For instance, in Tanith Lee's *Red as Blood*, the tale titled, "When the Clock Strikes," a retelling of "Cinderella," the protagonist of the tale recounts her version of the talewhere she claims that her version of the story is the truthful confession of the instances in her life. She says, "I hazard you have begun to recognise the story by now. I see you suppose I tell it wrongly. Believe me, this is the truth of the matter" (*Red as Blood* 54). This implies that the classical rendition of the fairytale is a crafted narrative where Cinderella is portrayed as a victim and innocent maiden, whose dependency is portrayed as a virtue and her passivity is celebrated as a cardinal trait of an ideal woman. On the contrary, in the retold version of the fairytale, the protagonist Ashella is no longer a victim or a passive receiver of favours rather she is the embodiment of female power. She avenges her mother's death in a most unorthodox way. She invokes satanic power and, finally, she succeeds in her mission. Though she takes an unconventional way to seek justice, Tanith Lee focuses on her determination and perseverance to seek justice, instead of accepting the situation she is forced to endure. Retold fairytale breaks the imposed passivity and dearth of power, which was "functional for maintenance of an oppressive power" (Eagleton 24-25).

The concept of 'external beauty' is one of the prominent traits demanded of the heroines in the classical fairytale, where their beauty outsmarts their knowledge and other skills they possess. The classical tales engrain an idea that women with external grace and beauty is more likeable and preferred than the one with knowledge. Meeta Rani Jha, commenting on the conventional representation of beauty and the underlining motive, says:

> An analysis of beauty is important because beauty can be converted into forms of social, economic, and symbolic power that devalue and denigrate some physical features while idealising and privileging others. More specifically, beauty functions as a symbolic marker of cultural and moral superiority in a hierarchy of racialised difference assigning goodness, godliness, intelligence, competence, and feminity to whiteness (5).

The make-believe conception about external beauty is subverted in the retold version of the tale. Though Ashella is beautiful, her interest is more than what the conventional protagonist will dream: "She is not like other girls. Despite her great beauty, she professed no interest in marriage, and none in clothes or jewel. She preferred to read in the garden at the foot of the tower" (*Red as Blood* 49). The classical role of the protagonist is counterpoised with the depiction of the protagonist in the mininarrative.

Classical tales advocated the social limitation for women to care only about trivial vanities like beauty, fancy dresses, dancing ball, banquets, household chores, etc. As they imparted the notion that "the beautiful girl does not have to do anything to merit being chosen; she does not have to show pluck, resourcefulness, or wit; she is chosen because she is beautiful" (Liebermann 188). But, mininarratives broaden their realm concerning knowledge, power and independence. The assumptive truth that is engraved in the minds of the reader about the classical rendition of "Cinderella," is distorted in such a way that the cultural and societal expectancy of women is challenged. Though she is beautiful in her regard, she was not known for her beauty. Mininarratives deconstruct the exalted portrayal of beauty and its make-believe significance in thc talc. As she tries to hide her beauty:

> People forgot her beauty. She was at pain to obscure it. She slunk about like an aged woman, a rag pulled over her head, dirt smeared on her cheeks and brow . . . Two years passed. They mislaid her beauty altogether, and reckoned her ugly. They found it hard to call to mind who she was exactly (*Red as Blood* 52).

The retold fairytale subverts the classical concept which is known as the accepted truth. The retold fairytales trivialise the concept of absolute truth with other alternative truths. Ashella, in the retold narrative, is known for her power instead of her beauty: "Under the filth and grime she was, impossibly, more beautiful, although no one could see it. And there was . . . her power . . . her power was rising like a dark moon in her soul" (*Red as Blood* 53). This so-called absolute truth reconceived by the postmodern configuration as 'intersubjective agreement or solidarity' has ingrained a falsified notion about the identity of women in the society which is reflected through the narratives. This overturned inception about women and their role in society or in the narratives was not a natural or instinctual entity but a manipulated prevarication systematised for their benefits. The socially constructed notion of a woman's physical beauty and external attractiveness is an oppressing and subordinating patriarchal value that paves way for the commoditisation of women. As, Noami Wolf aptly comments on the 'beauty myth' saying, "the signification of external beauty was not about women, but it is about "men's institutions and institutional power" (13). The fairytale narrative is one effective medium that institutionalised or authorised these fabricated truths through its textual instantiation. The classical fairytales fostered this complicity through its prevaricate narratives that imported the prejudiced agreement as the truth. Postmodernism, through its narrative valorisation, divulges the non-existence of the metanarrative truth or absolute truth.

The constructedness of absolute truth and its evolution as an intersubjective agreement or solidarity is substantiated through narrative instances of retold fairytales. This imparts a strong notion that the truth is not an independent assortment or untainted noble entity rather a product of human fabrication to exert power and to seek control. For instance, the trope of 'evil witch' used in the traditional fairytale is usually portrayed as an embodiment of evilness and a harbinger of destruction. Most of the traditional fairytales like "Snow White," "Rapunzel" and "Hansel and Gretel" exemplify the same idea of the witch being the female and evil. The witch figure is never portrayed as a normal human being rather she is portrayed as a symbol of malevolence and darkness. This conception of female characters being the evil witch is engrained in the minds of the reader through the classical narratives. The naturalised imposition of the witches being the symbol of evil wipes away the other possibilities of them being good and untagged. However, the patriarchal bias and power politics are very evident in the construction of the witch trope. These stereotypes of witch created by intersubjective agreement paved the way for socially legitimated hostilities. The metanarrative that portrayed the trope of the witch with a restrictive composure as evil sources eventually instituted the idea as indisputable truth.

On the contrary, the retold fairytale disfigures the conventional trope of the witch by shattering the role fixity that ensues a confined understanding. The retold narratives do not eliminate the trope completely from the tales, instead, they alter their stereotypical depiction. Though the witches in the retold tale invoke power in unorthodox ways, they use it for a good cause. This way the imposed truth is debunked by the postmodern narrative. For instance, in Tanith Lee's "Red as Blood," the Witch queen is extricated from the role fixity and portrayed as a witch with good intentions. She almost sacrifices everything to save her stepdaughter from the clutches of darkness and also the land from the terror: "The hag, who had been the beautiful Witch Queen . . . [gave Bianca] the apple…a fragment of the flesh of Christ, the sacred wafer, the Eucharist. The Witch Queen drew her Bible to her and opened it randomly. And read, with fear, the words: Resurgat" (*Red as Blood* 33). This enforced an altered dimension to the trope and invalidates the established truth imposed by the metanarratives. Postmodernism, Barry writes, as an "exhilarating, liberating phenomenon … [is] the claustrophobic embrace of fixed systems of belief" (81).

The performativity of the characters in the traditional fairytale is dictated by socio-political formulations. Whereas, retold fairytale through postmodernism, disrupts the role fixity and uncages them from the social constraints "advocating a means of escaping imposed limits and prescribed identity" (Warner 24). The retold fairytale thwarts the role fixity by subverting dominant ideology. The retold fairytale does not altogether obliterate the role of stepmother or witch from the narrative. Instead, it gives an alternative perspective and emancipates the restrained representation. For instance, the role of the witch is always paralleled with evilness and darkness. Typecasting the witches with evilness and malicious appearance is a prototypical trait of the traditional fairytale genre. Women are always depicted as witches where the very "definition of a witch excluded males" (Levack 135). The traditional fairytale like "Snow White," "Rapunzel" and "Hansel and Gretel" has the trope of an evil witch that instils the stereotypical picture.

Witches are stereotyped into the character that brings death, darkness and evil omen. They are not portrayed as characters with free will and choice rather they are constricted to fulfil the role. Instead of the character playing the role, they are played by the role. As Philip Mayer clearly points out saying, "The witch does not exist in . . . own right; it is the judgment of society that creates . . . the image of witch, and pins this image down onto particular individuals" (54). This social and gender stereotype is deconstructed in Emma Donoghue's *Kissing the Witch*. In the tale titled, "The Tale of Kiss," the protagonist recounts her experience of how she was manipulated to become a witch which she does not intend to do. The protagonist leaves the village and goes to the cave near the headland to avoid the criticism of the villagers as she was a barren woman. But soon she was misunderstood as a witch with power. She says, "I know what they say about me: the gulls bring me all the gossip . . . Contrary to what you might have believed, I am no monster under my skirts. I grew up in a place much like this . . . when I was the age that you are now I was a girl like you . . ." (*Kissing the Witch* 207).

As the days passed, the villagers started leaving presents for her and started enquiring about their future and approached her for the remission of their sins. She says:

> I thought such goodness had never been known in the whole world. I thought these were presents freely given to keep a stranger from starving. How was I to know that they were payment in advance? . . . So it was a witch they were wanting. I laughed to myself . . . it was not an arduous job . . . power that came not from my own thin body or own taunt mind, but was invested in me by a village (*Kissing the Witch* 210, 211, 213).

These lines disclose the manipulative ways in which traditional narrative imposed stereotypical and falsified image. The retold fairytales demure the role from its classical functioning and trivialises it by exposing the reality and its mediated truth. One of the critics aptly comments on this function of postmodernism saying, "[It] made their presence felt by deconstructing 'grandnarratives' and by exposing notions of reality and truth as fictional construct" (Ravichandran xxxiii). The stereotype of the evil witch is distorted by restructuring the trope with reality and demounting preconceived classical notions. The retold fairytale with postmodern subversive strategy expounds on the nature of classical fairytale narrative and its role in imparting culturally stained knowledge. Retold fairytales through their innovative strategy forge a new dimension eroding all misconceived notion about gender standards. It also reiterates the idea that the concept of the witch being evil is a subjective judgment, not a universal standard or absolute truth. Retold fairytales also shatter the assumption that the witch and her actions are necessarily wicked.

Retold fairytales through their textual candour and transgression against the established order invalidate the supremacy of single absolute truth. This, in a way, enables an altered perception and authentication of the other possibilities as co-existent truths. This denies the absoluteness and authenticity of the single metanarrative truth. The retold fairytales through their postmodern creativity promulgate altered dimensions of truth and its functioning. The retold fairytales with postmodern sensibility reshape, "the archetype of [our] imagination" and "recast the bricks of our inner world" (Dunker 223). The retold fairytales capturing the postmodern temperament through its narrative nuances express its radical notions against the canonised conventions of the classical fairytales.

The retold fairytales not only deconstruct the conventional patterns but also reconstruct it to reflect the contemporary sensibility. This eventually changes readers' apprehension and challenges the customary assurance inferred through the classical narratives. Maria Tatar confers this influence of retold fairytales saying, the innovative retelling using various techniques and exceptional imagination "thwart our expectations," and have reinvested a revolutionary ideal, "with a powerful creative social energy" (238).

Works Cited

Barry, Peter. *Beginning Theory: An Introduction to Literary and Cultural Theory.* Manchester UP, 2009.

Cranny-Francis, Anne. *Feminist Fiction: Feminist Uses of Generic Fiction.* Polity P, 1990.

Donoghue, Emma. *Kissing the Witch: Old Tales in New Skin.* Harper Collins, 1997.

Dunker, Patricia. "Re-imagining the Fairy Tales: Angela Carter's Bloody Chambers." *Popular Fictions: Essays in Literature and History*, edited by Humm et al., Methuen, 1986.

Eagleton, Terry. *Ideology: An Introduction.* Verso, 2007.

Grenz, Stanley. J. *A Primer on Postmodernism.* William B. Eerdsmans Publishing Company, 1996.

Hutcheon, Linda. *The Politics of Postmodernism.* Routledge, 2002.

Jha, Meeta Rani. *The Global Beauty Industry: Colorisum, Racism and the National Body.* Rutledge, 2016.

Lee, Tanith. *Red as Blood: Tales of the Sisters Grimmer.* Wildside P, 1983.

Levack, Brian. P. *The Witch-hunt in Early Modern Europe.* Longman, 1995.

Liebermann, Marcia. "Someday My Prince Will Come: Female Acculturation through the Fairy Tales." *Don't Bet on the Prince: Contemporary Feminist Fairy Tales in North America and England*, edited by Jack Zipes, Methuen, 1986.

Mayer, Philip. *Witchcraft and Sorcery.* Penguin Books, 1970.

Ravichandaran, T. *Postmodern Identity.* RBSA Publishers, 2007.

Rorty, Richard. *Truth and Progress: Philosophical Papers,* vol. 3, Cambridge UP, 1998.

---. *Objectivity, Relativism and Truth: Philosophical Papers.* Cambridge UP, 1991.

---. *Philosophy and the Mirror of Nature.* Princeton UP, 1979.

Tatar, Maria. *Off with Their Heads! Fairy Tales and the Culture of Childhood.* Princeton UP, 1992.

Warner, Maria. *From the Beast to the Blonde: On Fairy Tales and Their Tellers.* Farrar, Straus and Giroux, 1994.

Wolf, Noami. *The Beauty Myth: How Images of Beauty are Used Against Women.* William Morrow and Company Inc., 1991.

Chapter 4

Rewriting the Ancient Epics for Propagating Ideology: A Study of Volga's *The Liberation of Sita*

Virender Pal

In the "Introduction" to M.T. Vasudevan Nair's *Second Turn*, V.C. Harris mentions that the novel came into being only because the writer was able to expand on the "pregnant silences" (XII) of the writer of *Mahabharata*. In the novel, the writer gives a new twist to *Mahabharata* and deconstructs the Arjun-centric reading of the text. In the novel, Nair convincingly portrays Bheema as the hero of the epic. The readers are also forced to accept his point of view. When the readers read the novel, they realise that they have been oblivious to the facts presented by Nair. Nair writes that the silence in the epic was left by Krishnadwaipayana for the later writers to work on.

What Nair calls 'silence' is termed as absence by Derrida (Habib 653). According to Derrida, writing is haunted by absence, and this unique quality of writing, compared to orality, allows the readers to interpret the texts as they like. In fact, when a writer writes a text and publishes it, s/he loses control over it, and the interpretation of the work depends on the readers. In other words, the absence of the author in a literary work leads to multiple interpretations of the work and adds depth to it. However, there is another aspect of this absence; this allows the readers to manipulate the texts in whatever way they want. This might lead to (mis) interpretation of the work. This absence or pregnant silence of the authors has allowed writers to come up with creative texts based on the original texts.

In India, for instance, the two epics *Ramayana* and *Mahabharata* have been the source of many literary works. These modern works sometimes even explore the minor characters of the epic. For instance, V.S. Khandekar's *Yayati,* originally written in Marathi, revolves around a minor character of *Mahabharata*. In some works, writers take liberties and present the humane side of the characters of bedeviled characters like Duryodhana. It is said that the original name of the much-hated character of *Mahabharata* was Suyodhana. It seems justified also because the prefix 'du' means terrible. It is clear that no parent would give a sinister name to their son. However, it is generally agreed that the name of Suyodhana was changed to Duryodhana by generations of readers. The character of Duryodhana has also been redeemed by V. Raghunathan in his novel *Duryodhana*. V. Raghunathan presents Duryodhana, not as an evil man, but as a man who had to do immoral acts to get his due. In the novel, Duryodhana appears as a sagacious prince and a brave warrior capable of loving his friends and brothers. In one of the Chapters, V. Raghunathan shows that Duryodhana knows his responsibilities as a ruler:

> The ruler's duties towards the subjects were well known. He had to be liberal, generous, charitable, honest, just and of high moral integrity; he had to be gentle, kind, and empathetic, with ears to the ground. He had an obligation to use the riches of the state exclusively for the betterment of his subjects (189).

When one reads the works like *Second Turn* and *Duryodhana*, one realises that these works are ideologically neutral. In other words, these works are not a reinterpretation of the epic; instead, they are only the retelling of the story from a different perspective. In *Second Turn*, for instance, M.T. Vasudevan Nair deconstructs the Arjun-entric reading of the epic. In fact, *Second Turn* is Nair's reading "against the grain" (Atkins 92). Similar is the case of Duryodhana, where the writer tries to present the villain of the epic as a man turned into evil by circumstances.

There are some creations based on the epics which are saturated with ideology. Althusser argues that "great works of literature do not express an ideology" (Cuddon, 495). This statement of Althusser may be true for the original epics, but ideology has certainly coloured the works of the writers like Iravati Karve and Volga. In fact, ideology provides them with ground to reinterpret the epics according to the convenience of ideology. In *Yuganta*, Iravati Karve depicts that the tragedy of *Mahabharata* occurs only because of the treatment meted out to women like Kunti, Gandhari, and Draupadi. Volga, on the other hand, is very vocal about the role of her ideology in her writing. In an interview, she asserts:

> Then in 1981, I quit left politics and turned to feminist politics. It was turning politics in my career. I took writing seriously as I felt obliged to write because no one was writing about feminism or from feminist perspectives in Telugu. So to introduce feminism and to take it to people, I felt I had to write (Kumar 122).

In the above statement, Volga makes clear that she writes only to propagate feminism. One of the essential stands of feminism is that the females are oppressed by the males, a victim:

> The female is the victim of the species. During certain periods in the year, fixed in each species, her whole life is under the regulation of a sexual cycle (The Oestrus Cycle), of which the duration, as well as the rhythmic sequence of events, varies from one species to another. (Beauvoir 49).

She further writes about the inferior status of females:

> Even when she is willing or provocative, it is unquestionably the male who takes the female – she is taken. Often the word applies literally, for whether by means of special organs or through superior strength the male seizes her and holds her in place; he performs the Copulatory movements; and among insects, birds and mammals, he penetrates her (Beauvoir 49-50).

Most feminist writers believe that women suffer "economic and cultural disadvantages" in the patriarchal society (Cuddon 274). The interpretation of the epic *Ramayana* by Volga is also coloured by this belief, but her stories contained in "The Liberation of Sita" must be treated not as an interpretation of *Ramayana* but as an independent creative work. This is because she uses the background of *Ramayana* and Sita as her protagonist in the stories, but there are so many incidents which have been imagined by her only. There are no hints of such incidents in the epic. These incidents have been inserted into the stories to foreground her concerns. In other words, it can be said that these stories have been rewritten with a purpose in mind; to justify the ideological moorings of the writer.

In her interviews, Volga has already mentioned that she started writing because she wanted to propagate the ideology of feminism. The epics are the best starting point to start his kind of endeavour because epics like *Ramayana* are part and parcel of the life of people. Older people often quote from *Ramayana* and *Mahabharta* to deliver a point home. That is why any reinterpretation or retelling of the story on the epics will have a more comprehensive effect among the reading communities. Volga's take on *Ramayana* is an attempt to penetrate deep among the reading communities. The stories were initially written in Telugu, and their translation into English shows that they have reached readers in other parts of the country.

In the first story of the collection, "The Reunion", Volga takes the issue of the honour associated with women. In the contemporary partition literature, it has been seen that women become the easy target to communicate with the men folk of the community. During the partition of the sub-continent, violence erupted, and the women became the target of this violence. Partition literature is full of such instances where the women were abducted and violated by the people of the other as well as the same communities (Manto 39). The parades of naked women were taken out (Sarna 179). All these nefarious deeds were done to communicate with the males of the community. Chaman Nahal, in his novel *Azadi* depicts the scene of such a naked parade, "They were all stark naked. Their heads were completely shaven; so were their armpits. So were their pubic regions....The bruises on their bodies showed that they had been beaten and manhandled". (297) These parades were carried out to heap ignominy on the men folk of the other community. The parades were inhuman, and the women were only the passive receivers of hatred and violence that is reserved for the men folk of their community.

In the first story of the book "The Reunion", Volga also seems to suggest the same for Surpanakha. In Volga's story, Surpanakha appears as a helpless victim of Rama and Lakshmana's 'Wicked Prank.' In the original epic, Surpanakha was presented as a vamp who irritates Rama and Lakshmana beyond the limit. In Volga's story, she is a victim, and her adversary in the original epic seems to sympathise with her. For Volga, the disfiguring of Surpanakha was not a simple event; rather, it was done with a purpose. The motive behind the disfigurement of Surpanakha was to provoke her brother, the mighty king Ravana:

> Do women exist only to be used by men to settle their scores? Rama and Lakshmana would not have done this to Surpanakha if they did not know that she was Ravana's sister. Rama's objective was to provoke Ravana; his mission to find cause to start a quarrel with Ravana, was accomplished through Surpanakha (4).

In the same story, Volga also brings another theme of nature versus nurture. Surpanakha represents what nature is and Sita represents nurture. The description of Surpanakha by Volga makes clear that she lives in the surroundings of nature: "Garlands of yellow ganneru around her neck. Bracelets of nilambara on her wrists. She was like a walking creeper in the bloom" (6). Sita compares herself with Surpanakha: "She looked curiously at my jewellery as if wondering why I burdened myself with all that metal, which has neither fragrance nor grace" (6).

In the above lines, Sita seems to be longing for a life seeped in nature. Here in the debate on nature versus nurture, Sita seems to take the side of nature. However, it must be kept in mind that Volga seems to further an argument that Rama's war in *Ramayana* was an endeavour to bring Aryan civilisation to the south. Sita's ornaments represent the craftsmanship that was developed by the civilisation of the north.

Volga herself, belonging to a southern state, seems to have fallen to the Aryan invasion theory. The theory propounded by the British and White historians maintains that the Dravidian race of the original inhabitants of the subcontinent was pushed towards the south by the invading Aryans. The story suggests that Rama and Ravana belonged to two different races and their fight was not for morality or for establishing Dharma; rather, it was a racial rivalry. The main aim of the fight was to establish Aryan civilisation over the southern landmass. In the story, Volga suggests that the physical features of both races are different. Surpanakha tells Sita:

> I was so proud of my beauty. You don't know how much I adorned my nose. The sharp nose of you, Aryans, looked strange to me. There's a beauty in the strangeness, too, of course. My nose was neither sharp nor flat. It was, I thought, exactly how Eshwar must have conceived the perfect nose in the beginning of creation (11).

The above passage seems to suggest a marked difference between the shapes of the noses of the Aryans and the Dravidians.

However, when readers critically think about the story written by Volga, they realise that there are many loopholes in her story. In the story, Surpanakha represents people living in the forest; then what about Ravana, who lived in a grand mansion made of gold? The craftsmanship of Lanka was more outstanding than the jewellers who had made jewellery for Sita. When one looks at this proposition, one realises that Surpanakha, as a forest dweller, cannot be pitched against Sita, who lived in a royal palace, because Ravana's palace was grander, more prosperous and more ornate. Similarly, Volga's story ignores the role of Hanumana, Sugreeva and Jamwant in the original story. Going by the descriptions in the original epic, these were the real forest dwellers who helped Rama in conquering Lanka. Volga seems to have missed the technical details of the original epic in propounding her ideology. Moreover, science and scientific studies of different populations have found that the influence of central Asia on the pre-existing gene pool was minor (Sengupta et al.). Similarly, another research carried out by Estonian Biocentre, and the University of Delhi concludes: "Our high-resolution analysis portraying the three ancient tribal populations strongly rejects any incoming genetic signal of large scale, recent (during the post-Neolithic) migration either of the present to the subcontinent" ("Indo-Aryan migration Theory rejected").

In the second story of the book "Music of the Earth", readers are introduced to a Rama, which the readers are unaccustomed to. This Rama in Volga's story appears to be a firm believer and upholder of patriarchy. The attitude of Rama is made clear through his comments on Ahalya:

> She smiled graciously like a goddess. Sage Vishwamitra interrupted then and, leading me away, told me her story. My heart turned bitter. I was sad to know that there was no character behind that beauty. Yet I could not forget her (19).

In the above passage, the readers are told that the character of Ahalya is not good. The story conveys that sage Vishwamitra also believed the same about Ahalya. However, Kaushalya, Sita's mother-in-law and Rama's mother have contradictory thoughts about Ahalya. She tells Sita: "The wife of Maharshi Gautam, child. An exceptional beauty with a noble character befitting her beauty. Unfortunately, she was accursed" (21). Kaushalya further tells her: "As you know, men consider women objects of enjoyment" (21). The narrative of Volga makes Rama a toy in the hand of patriarchy.

Rama is a deity for millions of people, a man par excellence, a warrior, a statesman, but here in the story, Volga turns him into an ordinary human being. In the story, he appears not as a benevolent warrior, but as a man out to kill "the aboriginals in the neighbourhood" (2.4). It is clear that Volga is not satisfied with propagating feminism only; rather, she also plays the theme of Aryan versus Dravidians. In this story, Rama is presented as an Aryan hero who espouses Brahminical Virtues. One of the Brahminical Virtues was to treat women as property. Ahalya tells Sita:

> His property, even if temporarily, had fallen into the hands of another. It was polluted. Pollution, cleanliness, purity, impurity, honour, dishonour – Brahmin men have invested these words with such power that there is no scope in them for truth and untruth. No distinction (26).

Volga twists the story to suit her end. In the stories of Volga, the war between Rama and Ravana is decided at the time of Rama's marriage with Sita. Even Rama's stay of fourteen years in the forest was according to a plan. Volga makes a clear distinction between the people residing in the North and the South. While trying to create awareness among the females about feminism, she seems to create a rift and tries to divide the people on racial lines. A writer has to be very conscious while writing. Especially while writing about epics that are read throughout the country. In the story, Volga writes that the war between Rama and Ravana was not really about the abduction of Sita. She mentions that even Suparnakha's nose and ears were cut with planning. This was done to provoke Ravana. Ravana abducted Sita as a retaliation measure and gave Rama a chance to fight against Ravana. If the readers go accordingly to Volga, then Ravana was the most significant obstruction in the spread of Arya Dharma in the south. Ravana was a mighty saint warrior, a devotee of Lord Shiva who lived in an opulent palace made of gold. Rama's Ayodhya was not a match for the city he lived in. In Southern India, Lord Shiva is known as 'Eshwar' as called by Suparnakha. If Dravidians and Aryans are different races, then how the victorious Aryans started worshipping the Gods of the defeated people? Even Rama worshipped Shiva before conquering Lanka. Rama and Ravana worshipped the same God then; how can they belong to different races? However, to prove her point, she overlooks many facts. In the story "The Sand Pot," she writes:

> The Kshatriyas he killed were those who did not observe Arya Dharma. He has firmly established Arya Dharma in the entire northern plains. When he got to know that I revere Arya Dharma, he was pleased. He accepted me as his heir and handed me the responsibility of spreading the dharma in the entire southern plain (45).

Volga tries to differentiate between Arya dharma because she thinks that Arya dharma or the northern people were patriarchal, where even a mother could be killed by her son on father's command:

> That too is part of Arya Dharma, I know. To blindly carry out a father's wish without thinking about justice or injustice. My son did the same thing. Your husband promised my son that he too would perform the same task and establish Arya Dharma among the other races in the country (47).

Volga in her enthusiasm to spread one particular ideology, indeed ignores many points. In her stories, she suggests that all the relations and bonds have been devised to oppress women. She even suggests that marriage is also an oppressive institution. When Sita asks Renuka: "But won't creation come to an end if there is no bond of marriage?" Renuka seems to suggest that there is no need for marriage among human beings. Renuka replies, "Why would it come to an end Sita? Many creatures take birth and grow in this forest. They have no marital bonds, do they? There are people of different tribes whose customs are different from yours" (53).

Here, Volga again deconstructs her own arguments. In the first story, readers observe that Suparnakha wanted to marry Rama; even Ravana was married to Mandodri. In pursuit of ideology, she forgets that if marriage was an oppressive system where man oppressed the wife, then Rama would never have gone to the forest. It must be kept in mind that it was Kaikyi who overpowered Dashrath, Rama's father, in sending him to the forest for fourteen years. In many cases, marriage may be oppressive, but it cannot be generalised as recommended by Volga. In twisting the incidents of the like describing a meeting between Surpanakha and Sita, she uses her artistic liberty, but there are places where she seems to contradict herself. For instance, Sita is a warrior and has been trained in the use of arms. This again indicates no difference between the sons and daughters in society. However, Volga's strategies are different. In order to glorify Sita, Renuka and Ahalya, the male counterparts must be demonised. In the stories, Rama appears to be a man with a fragile ego, a man who wants his wife to be frail and weak. He tells Sita that he wants to protect her. To this, Sita replies that she is capable of protecting herself. Hearing this Rama's face falls (71), and he tells Sita:

> As long as I am alive, you will never have to protect yourself. Such a situation must not arise. You must look towards me for protection. You must turn to my strong arms for my protection. If you take care of yourself, what am I for? Promise me that you will never do that (71-72).

Rama, in the stories, seems to be incarcerated in his own castle. Volga seems to suggest that he is incarcerated by Arya Dharma. However, one of the most significant problems that remains with this collection of stories is that the differentiation between Aryan Dharma and other Dharma is not clear. If Aryan Dharma was patriarchal, was there any other alternative culture available? If yes, then was it matriarchal? Volga writes about Aryan Dharma but does not give any options to the readers.

The stories also sometimes seem implausible when Rama tells Sita that she should not protect herself and depend on him for her protection. Does he mean that Sita should not do anything? Even Sita could get killed to satisfy Rama's male ego. Volga has written or rewritten the stories from *Ramayana* to propound a particular ideology, but ultimately the ideology remains, and stories lose themselves in the ideology. If Rama wanted a frail, weak wife, then why did he marry Sita at all? While writing the stories, Volga fails to answer so many questions. Instead of intertwining her ideology in the stories, she lets the ideology overpower the stories and ultimately, bland ideology remains.

When the readers look at other stories like *Second Turn*, they realise that such stories have not been written to propound an ideology, instead, they offer alternative readings of the epics and foreground the episodes which were otherwise ignored by the reading communities. The stories of Volga are different in this sense. For her, stories are only vehicles for forwarding her ideology. In other words, for her end is essential, the medium is not.

Works Cited

Atkins, G. Douglas. *Reading Deconstruction Deconstructive Reading*. The UP of Kentucky, 1983.

Beauvoir, Simone de. *The Second Sex*. Translated by H.M. Parshley. Jonathan Cape, 1953.

Cuddon, J.A. *The Penguin Dictionary of Literary Terms and Literary Theory*. Penguin Books, 1976.

Habib, M.A.R. *Modern Literary Criticism and Theory: A History*. Blackwell Publishing, 2005.

Harris, V.C. "Introduction." M.T. Vasudevan Nair *Second Turn*. Translated by P.K. Ravindranath. Macmillan, 1997.

"Indo-Aryan Migration Theory Rejected." *The Deccan Chronicle*. Jun 18, 2015. web.deccanchronicle.com/150618/nation-current-affairs/article/indo-aryan-migration-theory-rejected.

Karve, Iravati. *Yuganta: The End of an Epoch*. Orient Longman 2006.

Kumar, T. Vijay. "Volga: An Interview." Volga *The Liberation of Sita*. Translated by T. Vijay Kumar and C. Vijayasree. HarperPerennial, 2016.

Manto, Sadat Hassan. *Toba Tek Singh Stories*. Translated by Khalid Hassan. Penguin, 2011.

Nahal, Chaman. *Azadi*. Orient Paperbacks, 1998.

Raghunathan, V. *Duryodhana*. Harper Collins, 2014.

Sarna, Mohinder Singh. "The Parade." In *Savage Harvest*. Translated by Navtej Sarna.Rupa, 2013.

Sengupta, Sanghamitra, et at. "Polarity and Temporality of High-Resolution Y-Chromosome Distributions in India Identify Both Indigenous and Exogenous Expansions and Reveal Minor Genetic Influence of Central Asian Pastoralists." *American Journal of Human Genetics*, vol. 78, no. 2, 2006.

Volga. *The Liberation of Sita*. Translated by T. Vijay Kumar and C. Vijayashree. Harper Perennial, 2016.

Chapter 5

Dialectics of Mythological Echoes in Select Stories of Mahasweta Devi

Poonam Choudhary

Mahasweta Devi is the heroic individual who raised her voice to protest and registers her discontent and disenchantment with the way life is lived by people. She, too, like literary giants not only celebrates humanity but very poignantly criticizes injustices and oppression forced upon human beings. In her fiction, she protests vehemently against all kinds of barriers of the family, the east, the rituals, the sects, the groups, the party, the nation, the administration, etc. that divide men and dwarf their stature. The irony of the fate of these people is that for whom they till the land and work in sun and shower, those very people by their oppression made the life a challenge for them and it has to be met in every condition. All over the country, marginalised have been assigned a lower and subordinate position sometimes in the name of tradition and custom and sometimes due to sociological reasons. Yet, change being the law of nature, time in its flux and flow erodes even the hardest of traditions and strongest of customs. She raises her powerful voice against the exploitation of the poor and the weaker class. Moreover, writer's sympathy for the poor and the oppressed is so acute that these stories became the mouthpiece of the anguished soul against the injustice common in those days.

In her short stories, Mahasweta Devi exposes the social evils like child-widowhood, poverty and prostitution. The present social system is a kind of service towards underprivileged. The tragedy of the exploitation of the landless peasant in India, and particularly in West Bengal, is an ageless one. So is the history of revolt, from the terrorist sanyasis and the indigo cultivators to the *Naxalbari* explosion. The people near Naxalbari in North Bengal are mostly tribal–the Medis, Lepchas, Bhutias, Santhals, Orangs, The zaminadars extend the petty bait of paddy seeds, the oxen team, a handful of rice and negligible wages. In return, they reap a lion's share of the harvest, at the cost of the landless labourer's back-breaking toil. Mahashweta Devi's struggle is to expose this story of exploitation.

Like history, Mythology has a tendency to repeat and reinvent itself. In order to comprehend the contemporary world, the modern writer seeks a parallel in the remote past. Mahasweta Devi's short story "Draupadi" revisits the past and recreates the character of the mythical Draupadi to formulate an account of a helpless woman who must fend for herself unlike the epical Draupadi who had Lord Krishna as her saviour. The beginning of the story reminds us of the mythical incident of the ill fate of Draupadi when she is born from an *Agni Kunda* as an addendum to his brother Dhrishtadyumna. She was firstly turned down by her father Drupada for he only considered his son Dhrishtadyumna to be worthwhile for his revenge with sage Dronacharya. She was accepted on the terms that the boon of Drupada would only work with her acceptance and that she would play an important role in the politics of Aryavarta (India) later on. As Draupadi became indispensable in the politics of Aryavarta, so it is the role of Dopdi Mejhen who is the protagonist and plays a significant role in the story.

The migrants like Dopdi or her husband Dulan Majhi, in Mahashweta Devi's short story "Draupadi", are forced to work for wages well below the government fixation of minimum wages. Even here, the greater tragedy is that gender bias leads to wage discrimination against woman labourers, and their exclusion from developmental programmes.

It is to the landlord's advantage to have the peasant evicted from his land for repayment of petty debts during droughts. This is because the landlord is himself the moneylender. Mahashweta Devi's stories are pitched against the background of this struggle. Documentation is never far from narrative here. The Government remained committed to eradicate the struggle and shoot down the fervent student – leaders of the Naxalite movement. Brati in *Hazaar Churashir Ma* (The Mother of 1084) is indoctrinated in the '*vrata*' of fighting the cause of the exploited in the slums of Calcutta. Student activists Anindya and Malini in *Agnigarbha* (The Womb of Fire) fight to provoke the landless Santhals like Dopdi, Dulna and Boshai Toodoo in the art of guerrilla warfare against the zamindar and the police. But basically, Mahashweta Devi's peasant mutineers are neither Naxalites nor Communists. This is because she firmly believes that whatever the manifesto of party-politics and banners proclaim authority and authority alienates instinctively. Moreover, like all revolutionaries, the basic instinct of a rebel like Bashai Tudu, the repeatedly regenerated santhal in *Agnigarbha*, is to find answers to his own problem. His argument – the Naxal may be prepared to die for the peasant movement, but can the educated Naxalite or the gentleman Communist experience the tragedy of the landless Santhal, subsisting on roots, rats and spiders in times of drought?

Often, in Mahashweta Devi's stories, a tension exists between two worlds: the world of destitution and poverty where the woman is accepted in her elemental roles and that of upper class avarice and debauchery, where her beauty and image are exploited. There is a strong unity in the tribal society which cancels out the conventional frontiers of feminism. It is only in the upper echelons of society that a Kowsalya can degenerate into a political cliche, a Dopdi be raped, a Jahnavi sold piece by piece. Within the tribal society, however, a woman's honour remains inviolate.

The silent tears of the daily struggle are presented to us in the startling rawness of the language. It is the rural diction at its best, with its strong dialectical flavour, its violent images. The major portion of Mahasweta Devi's creative writings has been devoted, particularly, to expose the inhuman subjection of women and their struggle for survival. They do not conform to any school of feminism and suffer in male dominated society. In the comparison to men, women become "the softest target for the great upholders of the traditional values" and are subjected to all kinds of humiliations and, finally, are compelled to lose their identity. Her protagonists do not yield to the forces of the society in which they live. Rather, they struggle hard to make their mark by exhibiting exemplary courage and moral strength even in the face of hostile climate of stifling conventions. Samik Bandyopadhyay comments in this connection:

Two classes of characters that have dominated Mahasweta Devi's stories and novels in the seventies are the mothers bearing the brunt of social and political oppressions, and enduring and resisting with indomitable will … they are too earthy and emotionally charged to bear overtones of any mystical–mythical or archectypal motherhood. They are invariably located within a network of relationships defining their personalities into absolute clarity (4). The bonded labour system, in fact, has its origin in the *Varna* (caste) system. Indian society had been stratified into four castes – *Brahmin, Kshtriya, Vaishya* and *Shudra.* The people belonged to the caste of *Shudra* were denied rights to property, education and choicc of occupation. They were made to depend either on the feudal lords or landowners for their livelihood. Indian Government permitted the feudal land system to remain unaffected in rest of the nation. The upper caste landlords are still as feudal as they were abiding by values which are against women and the lower castes. For the last fifty years, one India has remained basically feudal while the other has remained an object of class and caste subjugation.

The Estate Acquisition Act of 1954 forbade acquisition of more than 25 acres of land. It was followed by the Rural Land Ceiling Act of 1971. Despite these government gestures, exploitation and cruelty continued unabated, reaching its worst depths in the Tea Garden of North Bengal in 1959. It sparked off the revolt of bonded labourers in 1968 and the Naxalbari movement from 1967 onwards. Mahasweta Devi's stories are pitched against the background of this struggle. The poor victims had to accept the most degrading terms and agreed to work under the most unfavourable and unpleasant conditions imposed on them by the masters. She should confine herself by and large to a certain section of society whose welfare was her main concern. Her stories specialise in painting the miseries, disabilities, humiliations and the various types of exploitation, which has been the lot of poor, suppressed and exploited sections of Indian society.

Formally, bonded labour was abolished in November 1975. Since little was done by the state government for these rehabilitations, the landless ex-bonded labourers came in acute distress and at this crucial time the agents of various masters took the advantage of opportunity and lured them away to the places with promises of good Jobs. Mahasweta Devi brings forth this picture in her activist writings as well as in her fictional world. She states, "The land given to the freed bonded labourers is uncultivable, the good land is held by the master, though the ownership – paper is in the freed labourer's name. There is no water for drinking or irrigation; no chance of being employed by government agencies for roads – repairing, timber felling, etc."(5).

Mahasweta Devi has presented a realistic picture of rural India and its barbaric system of bonded labour. *Outcast* is the collection of four stories namely "Dhouli," "Sanichari," "The Fairy Tale of Rajbasha," and "Chinta," With all the vehemence and skill at her command, Mahasweta Devi champions the cause of the underdog of Indian society. In her stories, we see simple human souls fated against the soulless poverty of industrialisation. Dhouli and her mother's estrangement offer Mahasweta Devi an opportunity to examine lives in and out of the society. They live in a world in which women must not survive without men. "Dhouli" is undoubtedly a manifesto of exploitation. Unlike her literary predecessors, who placed their female protagonists within narrow, apolitical social frameworks, Mahasweta perceives women's oppression as linked to larger issues of social exploitation.

Dhouli, the protagonist, becomes the focus of the mingled love and hatred engendered by the family of her lover. When Misri Lal leaves Dhouli after the physical reunion, she suffers from mental disorder and she considers the relief that may come only after her death. But as she realises that she is pregnant, she could not dare to kill her unborn child and, being a tribal girl, wraps herself in the tribal women's motherhood and heroism. Mahasweta Devi describes her as strange and dangerous. Dhouli is an acutely sensitive and defiant woman whose non-conformity is a living criticism on the dreadful lives of her mother and of her own.

The wheel of Dhouli's fortune runs so fast in the opposite direction that till the innocent girl of twelve could understand the meaning of the things, she finds everything shattered into pieces. The condition of Dhouli becomes worse in the story. First, she suffered when she was married in her childhood to the person whom she doesn't know. She could barely understand the meaning of marriage when she becomes a widow of a man for whom she never feels any emotional attachment. She suffers due to her poverty, caste discrimination, the age old tradition of early marriage of a girl in tribal classes, and the worst calamity which befell on her as the death of her husband at a young age. She becomes nostalgic of going to *mela* riding on her father's shoulder while regretting not going to *nautanki*. She is destined to wear coarse, dull plain black cloth, "and slaving on the mahajan's farm or the folder's field" … on top of that, a child too? No, she did not want such a life" (4). She is destined to lead a life of widow to whom everything good of the world is denied: "After becoming a widow, a randi, you were not supposed to look in a mirror. Not supposed to look at yourself. Not supposed to wear shellac bangles, a dot of sindoor on your forehead, anklets of cheap metal, she was attractive. But a pretty face was no use to a randi" (5).

At this critical juncture of her life, she is proposed love by Missilal, a Brahman boy which starts a tale of unending miseries in her life. She suffers a great mental conflict and ultimately devices to accept his love as he; "At a glance you could make out that he was a deota. And what was Dhouli? A dusad's daughter. A widow. An unfortunate woman. She had no father or brother, which was why Kundan had not let her mother till the land" (6). And moreover, low-caste women have no right to love a man of the upper class rather it is a sin on her part. Unfortunately she commits the same sin. Though in her heart the fear is working that his love may not be merely a play. She is bold enough to share her fear with Mishrilal. She says "It's you? ... Dusadin, don't you understand what love mean?" (8).

The condition worsens when Dhuoli comes to know that she is going to be an unmarried mother of Mishrieal's son. Even in the eyes of a mother (a woman herself) the honour of family is more significant than a girl's chastity. Their illegitimate children wondering here and there were the result of their illegal relations with these down-trodden women, Dhouli's mother says to Dhouli: "They always make such promises. You're not the first dusad girl the Misra has ruined. Dusad, ganju, dhobi who have they spared?" (59).

Mahasweta Devi's purpose in showing us the psychic state and the resultant behaviour of Dhouli, under the pressure of Misra's domination, is to expose the vicious effect of racism on the gangu, dhobi and dusad girls, thereby raising the question of what it means to be tribal and poor. Even if we do not see ethnicity as a mask behind which people and their class position both from each other and from themselves, even if we realise the importance of racial and ethnic values, we are forced to suffer due to class distinction.

Things that came from her pen were something new and quite real, as no woman writer had ever before written with such power and honesty. She recognises the inadequacy of male created ideologies and struggles for the spiritual, economic, social and racial equality of women sexually colonised and biologically subjected. She gives expression to the mute and stifled female voice denied an equal freedom of self-expression. It is a concept emerging as a protest against male domination and the marginalisation of women. Sarah Grimke observes: "Man has subjected women to his will, used her as a means to promote his selfish gratification, to minister to his sensual pleasure, to be instrumental in promoting his comfort, but never has been desired to elevate her to that rank she was created to fill. He has done all he could do to debase and enslave her mind" (19).

In "Dhouli", Mahasweta Devi creates a character that seeks identity for himself in a world which has for ages suppressed his kind. The protagonist Dhouli confronts a society that denies her to live a life of an equal human being. She is destined to do the work she hates. The innocent people still experience the trauma of inhuman subjugation by the landlords who reign supreme in the village. In an interview with Gyatri Chakraborty spirak, Mahasweta Devi reflects, "The bonded labour system survives. The bonded labour system was introduced by the British. They created a new class, which took away tribal land and converted the tribals into debt bolnded slaves" (1).

Another mythical character that we encounter is Sanichari, an orphan girl, who is forced to work in the bricklins. She describes women as the most exploited and oppressed section of the entire working class. They are exploited as workers in the field and at home. Being an activist Mahasweta Devi possesses a deep and keen knowledge of historical, political and sociological movements and of their brutal leaders lurking behind the main plots and themes of her all creative writings. Gyatri Chakrborty Spivak remarks, "And the major event that occurred after she had become a professional writer, in the late sixties and early seventies, was the Naxalite uprising which seemed to have exerted a tremendous influence on her writings. The target of these movements … easily circumvented the law" (6).

Whenever there is famine or drought, survival and livelihood for these people become a question not to be solved without the help of these *malik* and taking the benefit of their helplessness, they become their gods. Their women can survive on fruits and roots from the forest but they need money also for the other things of life. The ex-concubine of the kiln owners becomes the recruiting women and is called *sardar*. The dire necessities of their life easily make them their prey as told by Mahasweta Devi, "So it has been easy for the sardars to collect a willing batch of girls, bribe the police, railway police and the political parties, and bring the girls to Calcutta"(2).

If anyone refuses to act accordingly then every kind of torture is inflicted upon them. They are forced to live in a very miserable and troublesome condition as remarked by Mahasweta Devi in her activist writings:

> These unfortunate beings live in Jhopris worse than pig-holes. There are no sanitary arrangements, nor any drinking water where they work through the summer days. The kiln is closed with the one set of the monsoons and the *rejas* are sent home (4).

Mahasweta Devi links up the story of Sanichari with the Raksha Morcha meeting. Drought makes those four girls a prey to Gohuman and two years later it was Raksha Morcha meeting which forces this group of girls to give themselves up Gohuman's fangs voluntarily. The issue like police-struggle-violence-adivasi-raksha morcha apparently has nothing to do with Sanichari's tale but the link between the Raksha Morcha meeting and Sanichari meeting Gohuman is both real and strong. Raksha Morcha meeting set things ablaze and the police and BMP took over Rata and its adjoining areas and a reign of terror is unleashed in the entire area. Mahasweta depicts the terror, "It's inhuman. They have devoured all the poultry and goats. Smashed the ploughs, Destroyed whatever few possessions there were. Pots and pans, hunts, all razed to the ground" (2).

Sanichari's plight is an ironic representation of our society's ruling that creative space must be discovered within those relationships which have the sanction of society. Any attempt to extend its rigid boundaries can only result in misunderstanding and misery. One should not, however, fail to understand that Sanichari suffers not only because of caste but also because of her feminine gender. She finds herself in a double jeopardy of race and gender. As a racial being, she is asked to relinquish her individual and cultural ways and follow kilns owners and, as a female, she is socialised to subordinate her femininity and remain subsumed in the orbit of patriarchy.

In "The Fairy Tale of Rajabasha," Mahasweta Devi attempts to give an artistic expression to the sufferings of the under-privileged class, tribals, adivasis in their confrontation with the powerful exploitative mechanism which, according to Samik Bandypadhyay, "operates beyond the law and with the tacit acquiescence of an exploded class held in thrall by a load of conventional role obligations. Legal reforms or legal defenses for the exploited have rarely affected the exploitation mechanism sustained by the illiteracy/ignorance of the exploited" (7).

"The Fairy Tale of Rajabasha," is a story of the Ho tribe that gets sucked into the racket of contractors of *maal* who were transported to Punjab. It presents the realistic picture of rural India where the barbaric system of bonded labour has been at work. The bonded labour system, in fact, it has its origin in the caste system. The people belonged to the lower caste were denied to have land education and choice of occupation. They were made to depend on others for their survival. Their total dependence on the upper classes reduced their status to that of slaves. Even today most of the labourers belong to this section of the people. N.D. Kamble rightly states:

> In practice banded labour in India is the culmination of the debtor-creditor relation into slave and master relation. But bonded labour is an outcome of the socio-economic system prevailing in India. Some people who were deprived of the socio-economic and political powers had to depend on those who enjoyed these powers. Criminal poverty of vulnerable sections exposed them to exploitation in the built in mechanism of socio-economic system. Economic dependence and poverty of the under – privileged sections of the society forced them to be slaves (29).

Mahasweta Devi's outlook and perception of the life of the suffering humanity gives the story a new dimension. In her capacity as an active social worker and journalist, Mahasweta Devi has come out into contact with the lives and struggles of the under-privileged and lower class communities settled in the border regions of the three neighbouring states – West Bengal, Bihar and Orissa. She has been a witness to many pathetic incidents in their lives.

Joshmina in "The Fairytale of Rajabasha", become the symbol of the ultimate exploitation of women as woman – an exploitation of her nurturing body while the society shirks all responsibilities for the terrible consequence. Mahaweta's sympathetic description of the incident has been charged with a sense of authenticity. Thus the story deals with female circumcision not from the feminist point of view, as the control of female sexuality, but from a humanist and progressive one. It leads us to understand the irony of male insistence on female rites as displaced importance and as ultimately deconstructive.

Mahasweta Devi is one of our literary personalities who is committed to the cause of restoring human values. She displays total sincerity, unflinching commitment and a deep-seated urge to abolish the anomalies of existing socio-economic conditions. Her stories present an expression of her deepest concern about the retrograde conventionalities of modern society that make it a pull work of exploitative mechanism. She is motivated by a sense of history in depicting the life-like situations in contemporary society.

Works Cited

Beauvior, Simone De. *The Second Sex.* Translated by H.M. Parshley, Harmonds, 1974.

Bandyopadhyay, Samik. "*Introduction.*" *Five Plays.* Seagull Books, 1986.

Devi, Mahasweta. *Outcast: Four Stories.* Translated by Sarmistha Dutta Gupta. Seagull Books, 2002.

---. *Rakshi Kora.* Translated by Samik Bandyopadhyay.Hyderabad Books Trust, 1982.

---. *Preface to Shrestha Galpa*, Calcutta 1985.

Spivak, Gayatri Chakroborty. *Forewriting on Sexual Differences.* Edited by Elizabeth. Alse. Stanford. 1982.

Chapter 6

Untold Sagas of Kunti's Motherhood: Rewriting the Myth in Tagore's *Karna Kunti Samvad* and G. Sankara Pillai's *Wings Flapping Somewhere*

Thejimol George

Myths and legends are a unique form of discourse deeply embedded in the society. They define and redefine the essential questions related to human existence throughout the ages. Right from the beginnings of human civilisation, mythological tales and characters exert an influence upon the respective social and cultural lives of the generation. These folk tales locate in the primordial memory of human beings and they have been emerging in numerous permutations and combinations over the ages undertaking new meanings, adaptations and digressions. In the modern literary scenario, mythical characters have played a decisive role in framing and generating certain attitudes and perspectives in scripting the roles of men and women in the society. Marina Warner comments:

> Myths offer a lens which can be used to see human identity in its social and cultural context . . . they can lock us up in stock reactions, bigotry and fear, but they are not immutable, and by unpicking them, the stories can lead to others. Myths convey values and expectations which are always evolving, in the process of being formed, but . . . and this is fortunate . . . never set so hard they cannot be changed again … (14).

With the advent of postmodernism, there was a tendency to redefine the mythological situations and characters and they began to reappear in the contemporary fictional world bearing multiple layers of meanings related to human identity. Indian sensibility is deeply rooted in the stories from our two great epics, *Ramayana* and *Mahabharata* which are an integral part of Indian culture and society. No wonder then, most of the characters like Draupadi, Kunti, Ahilya,

Manu, Yama, Bhim Sena, Karna, etc. reappeared in the literatures from the regional languages in India.

On the other hand, myth is a story transmitted orally through the generations. While passing from one generation to the other, it becomes an inexplicable part of the social consciousness and ultimately it becomes a general truth. Myths are symbolic of the accumulated knowledge of the society operating within the ideologies associated to it. Myths provide interpretative archetypes so as to define the present realities through the past. Roland Barthes rightly termed it as "metalanguage" because it is a second order language which is used to interpret and define the first order language. It functions as a signifier and in performing a signifying function myth "neither hides nor flaunts something, but it distorts; myth is neither a lie nor a confession: it is an inflexion" (129). Myth distorts reality and naturalises it; thereby transforming history into nature. In *Mythologies,* Roland Barthes uses the term myth as indicative of any fabricated or illusory thing, the distorted representations and invalid beliefs prevalent in the society which we accept as natural. Society always has atendency to naturalise the beliefs and ideologies in these myths. Since the mythological texts are epics recorded by men, they describe the heroic deeds of the protagonists and numerous characters are silenced/or forced to remain silent in the whole narrative. The deconstructive way of reading the texts digs up numerous layers of its meanings which are left unnoticed.

Deconstruction is a way of close reading the texts in order to demonstrate that any given text has irreconcilably contradictory meanings, rather than being a unified, logical whole. As the American critic Barbara Johnson described it, "The deconstruction of a text does not proceed by random doubt or arbitrary subversion, but by the careful teasing out of warring forces of signification within the text" (112). Deconstruction was created and has been profoundly influenced by Jacques Derrida, the eminent French philosopher. Derrida, who coined the term deconstruction, argued that in western culture people tend to think and express their thoughts in terms of binary oppositions. When this philosophical doctrine is applied to the realm of literature, it communicates multiple layers of meanings that can be produced within the text. For Derrida, there is nothing outside the text and the text itself is self-contradictory in nature. Apart from the tenets of New Criticism and Formalism that the text is a unified single whole, Derrida argued in his theory of difference a point of 'undecidability" and the text undermined its own rhetorical structure, dismantles or deconstructs it. This way of reading challenged the existing interpretive paradigms and dismantled the naturalised truths transmitted through the folk tales/songs, mythological stories and *Puranas*. It opens up new avenues of reconstructing the past in accordance with the contemporary social and cultural ideologies. Here, the observations of Linda Hutcheon on re-vision of past could be taken into consideration, "By recalling the texts of the past . . . of literature or even of history . . . postmodern novels similarly use parody to question whether there can ever be such a thing as a final definitive "inscription" of selfhood or subjectivity in fiction" (8).

Numerable writers from the Indian subcontinent gave expression to the marginalised characters from these epics and the present paper examines the portrayal of Kunti, being the mother of the Pandavas and of Karna (her first born yet abandoned son) as represented both in Rabindranath Tagore's *Karna Kunti Samvad*, a dramatic poem on Kunti's motherhood and G. Sankara Pillai's *Wings Flapping Somewhere,* a dramatic monologue on psychological conflicts in Kunti as a mother. Focused on the pangs of Kunti and on the psychological miseries that she undergoes, these two literary pieces foregrounded the unseen and unheard stories of the mother of the Pandavas.

The Indian notion of womanhood has been largely shaped on India's two great Epics *Mahabharata* and *Ramayana*. Both the texts are full with women characters that represent every facet of womanhood. These characters of the epics are loaded with different layers of human existence and multiple modes of human consciousness which make it possible for every age to discover a new layer. It is the only reason that in recent times the portrayal of the dynamic and assertive women characters has been taken up into consideration. It is in this context that a study of contemporary representation of Kunti is relevant and possible.

In Vyasa's *Mahabharata*, Kunti is seen as a strong-willed and powerful figure who acted as a pillar of strength for the Pandavas even in the times of distress. Though she is a rigorous follower of *Dharma*, a dutiful wife and an affectionate mother, she is an isolated woman. The boon given by the sage Durvasa and the subsequent incidents in Kunti's life form the warp and weft of *Mahabharata*, the great epic, and she emerges as a strong woman. Kunti invoked the Sun – God and she gave birth to the child unimpaired her chastity. Afraid of the stigma and shame of the society, she kept it a secret and took the most accursed decision in her life, to set adrift the son and abandoned her child in the silence of the night on the banks of the river Ashva. This act of hers ruined Karna's life, degrading him from a *kshatriya* to *sutaputra*, as he was looked after by Athiradha, the Charioteer of the King of Hastinapur and Radha. Even though Kunti regretted taking the decision of giving up the baby in silent grief and guilt, she was afraid of the shame of being an unwed mother in the society. The psychological ferment, out of this grief and guilt, in Kunti's motherhood found elegant expressions in Tagore's *Karna Kunti Samvad* and G. Sankara Pillai's *Wings Flapping Somewhere.*

Karna Kunti Samvad is a dramatic poem taken from Rabindranath Tagore's poetic collection *Kahini* (1900) and translated into English by Ketki Kushari Dyson. The work is a re-reading of the *Udyogaparva* of Mahabharata. It is a story of encounter between a fostered son and a natural mother set against the backdrop of the eve of the Kurukshetra war. Tagore's portrayal of Kunti and Karna is much different from Vyasa's epic heroes. They are more human beings in Tagore's dramatic poem. The secret pangs of motherhood are central to Tagore's *Karna Kunti Samvad.* Tagore portrays a more humanised Karna and a despairing mother, who is longing for her lost child. In *Mahabharata*, Kunti met her first-born yet abandoned son when he was finishing his late morning prayers by the sacred river Jhanavi. The river Ganges is called by this name at the point of its origin from the Himalayan hills. She waited anxiously and eagerly so as to meet him personally in the burning heat at the noon. On the contrary, Tagore made the meeting possible in the glow of twilight deepening into a starlit night. This serene and tranquil rendezvous between the mother and son itself proclaimed the human emotions embedded in it. Karna, imbibing the vigorous energy of the youth just like the impetus and swift river Jhanavi, introduced himself:

> ...Karna is my name,
> Son of Adhirath the charioteer, and Radha is my mother.
> That's who I am (*Karna Kunti* 2-4).

At the very outset of the poem, Karna introduced himself as the son of Adhirath, the charioteer of the king of Hastinapur and Radha. His emphasis on the "*suta*" lineage is a deliberate dramatic intervention by Tagore to highlight the contrast between his belief that he is the son of a common charioteer and reality of his noble birth. Also in the epic, even before the Kurukshetra war, Karna was aware of his birth and the related stories from Lord Krishna. Tagore, interested in making a different kind of audience impact, made Karna hear about who his natural mother is from her own mouth, thus making the encounter much more meaningfully dramatic. When Karna addressed himself as the son of Adhirath, Kunti immediately disclosed the very truth to him:

> Child, in the first dawn of your life
> It was I who introduced you to this wide world
> That's me, and today I've cast aside
> All embarrassment, to tell you who I am (*Karna Kunti*5-8).

Kunti expressed her long-lost love for Karna. She recalled the day in the arena of Kurukshetra war when her first born son was insulted despite his noble lineage. On the day of the tournament, he entered the battlefield like the "newly rising sun" and Kunti was eagerly waiting to see him. When Kripa, the martial instructor, asked his father's name to Karna, he added that one who is not born of a royal family has no right to challenge Arjun at all. Karna was so insulted and humiliated by the incident that he was reddened with shame. Kunti saw her son speechless with his face lowered down. At the same moment, Duryodhana crowned him as the Prince of Anga and rescued him from the stigmatised identity. At the moment, she too wished to hug her son but she couldn't.

In *Udyogaparvam*, Karna, a rigid follower of *dharma* is more sharp and outspoken to his mother. He shows his fidelity to the Kauravas even though he knew well that the Pandavas will win the war. He actually offers Kunti the assurance that he will not kill all her sons. Tagore's treatment of the characters is more psychological and humane. Tagore's characters are succumbed with human emotions such as agonies, miseries, dubious stands, conflicts, resentments and so on. The epic hero Karna is humanised to suit the tastes of Tagore's own times. Tagore's Karna was deeply moved by the grief-stricken words of the distressed mother. The affection between mother and son is articulated vividly in Tagore's poem. Kunti craved to take him to her "thirsty bosom" and to her "maternal lap" so as to love him (*Karna Kunti* 65). For him, a mother's lap is a sanctum, a sacred place that cannot be gambled away.

It was known to him that he was given up by his natural mother, but in the dreams of his nights he longed to see the mother in reality. Owing to the bewilderment of his situation, karna became more humane and the filial love towards his mother generated a great dilemma in him. Kunti wished Karna to be sided with the Pandavas in the war and she beseeched to him. Suddenly, Karna too entered into an illusion and promised to Kunti that he would always be with her. His long cherished dream had now turned into a reality and her call had awakened his soul. No longer was he able to hear the drums of battle and everything related to the battle seemed false to him. Tagore's Karna is quite different from the epic hero Karna in the *Udhyogaparva* of *Mahabharata* as Tagore presents the mental agonies, sufferings and humiliations of Kunti's abandoned child. Karna rather than the heroic figure. He wavers in the middle of their conversation, is flooded with nostalgia and filial affection to be anointed by his mother's love, and then immediately retreats to a noble resolve.

Tagore's characters are more human beings who undergo a conflict in their mind rather than gallant warriors. Human emotions of motherhood and filial love add to both the crisis and the sublimity of the dramatic poem. Kunti called him back to her thirsty bosom, to her maternal lap and this long-lost feeling of motherhood is recurred in the poem. Tagore focuses on Kunti as a deprived mother whose "heart is childless" though she mothered five sons (*Karna Kunti* 158). She felt emptiness in her womb as she cast aside her first born, Karna. The action of discarding the child was equivalent to committing hundred crimes, so she beseeched his forgiveness and let that forgiveness burn fiercer than any rebukes within her breast. Forgiveness burning fiercer than rebukes is a very noble thought and highlights the tenderness of relation between the mother and the son. Karna was melted down by her pleadings. She offered him the privilege of being her elder son and being the king of Hastinapur.

Though Karna was deeply moved by the words of Kunti, he recovered his true identity as a warrior among the Kauravas. Addressing Kunti as mother, he took pride in his *suta* lineage and considered it his most glorious identity:

> The riches from which you disinherited me
> Cannot be returned – it's beyond your powers.
> When I was born, Mother, from me you tore
> Mother, brothers, royal family – all at one go. (*Karna Kunti* 192-195)

Towards the end of their conversation, Karna gave an assurance to Kunti that the Pandavas would win the war and they would reign the country. Karna waited intently for a heroic death with the losers in the battle:

> Let me stay with the losers, those whose hopes will be dashed.

> The night of my birth you left me upon the earth:
> Nameless, homeless. In the same way today
> Be ruthless, Mother, and just abandon me:
> Leave me to my defeat, infamous, lustreless. (*Karna Kunti* 222-226)

G. Sankara Pillai is an Indian playwright, critic and director, noted for his contributions to modern Malayalam theatre. He was an experimental writer who synthesised both the traditional and modern techniques in his plays. *Wings Flapping Somewhere* is a dramatic monologue with Kunti as the protagonist. Revolving around the subtle psychological conflicts of Kunti as a mother, the play is rich in its profound symbols. The fervent symbol of an unknown and unseen bird and the flapping sound of its wings are recurring motifs in the play. It reverberates her past and Kunti's representation in the play undergoes numerous transitions and each phase represent different facets of her life. She traversed through the phases as a young girl, an unwed mother, wife of Pandu, mother of Pandavas and the playwright focused more on the psychological conflicts she had to encounter being an unmarried mother. As the traditional Indian plays, *Wings Flapping Somewhere* too begins with an invocation to the God of Agni, which is the most powerful and magnificent element of nature. Glorious Agni exists in many forms in the play too and, moreover, Kunti got pregnant by the God of Sun as per the boon granted by the sage Durvasa. Despite being a princess and a mother of the God's child, she had to abandon the first born son because of her fears in the society.

The play begins with the monologue of the actress, who later metamorphosed into Kunti, imbibing the blazing spirit of Agni and criticizing the plight of contemporary women in our society who is not able to break the chains of the marital knot even if it suffocated them. Then she reappeared on the stage as Kunti, looking bewildered and listening to the flapping of the wings of the bird which called her by her name Pritha. That was "how I was called…Pritha…Like someone who is very close to me – like a whisper and then, then wings flapping… and the notes of a long bird call" (*Wings* 72). This bird and its wing beats that brushed past her and remained a constant presence in Kunti's life. But it was invisible to her, a reality that always evaded her. Amidst all the din and bustle of the Kurukshetra war and the coronation festivities of the Pandavas, she couldn't avoid its ghostly presence.

With the flapping sound, she was reminded of the glorious victory of the Pandavas in the Kurukshetra war, yet haunted by the miserable past in her life. The invisible bird and its long call is a recurrent motif in the play which evoke the psychological trauma in Kunti's motherhood. She recollected the very first night when she heard this bird call, when she abandoned the child at the banks of the river. She traversed through the different phases in her life as the young luscious woman being lured by the Sun God, the light of the world and got pregnant by the Lord. After giving birth to the baby, she was devastated, wishing to throw the baby away in the middle of the night. But, she says, it was "on that day, for the first time, that I heard this bird's cry, the indistinct flapping of its wings, as the movement, the sound, of distances" (*Wings* 75).

Kunti recalled the night when she had given up the child out of the stigma and shame from the society. She laid the baby in a broken box and it was floating in the water and she could listen to the bird's cry as a sobbing, "I haven't forgotten it… I could never ever forget it" (*Wings* 76). The tumult in her life is vocalised in this play with the symbolic presence of the bird. It appears whenever Kunti is in distress.

Tagore's poem and G. Sankara Pillai's play drew some parallel connections where Kunti is reminded of the day when Karna was insulted by the Pandavas and how Duryodhana anointed him the King of Anga. She was forced to witness her sons fighting with each other, "all this enervated only one a mother my own sons fighting on both sides…against each other…and I…this miserable creature…incapable of giving advice" (*Wings* 78). The play evokes the futility of war as it is reflected in Kunti's mind after the Kurukshetra war that it is a ground filled with mutilated bodies.

One of the intrinsic moments in the play is when Kunti is interfered by a superhuman figure with a half mask covering the face, and the white, spread out clothes hanging loose from the arms like wings. The masculine figure invigorates the condemned self of Kunti's motherhood. After the Kurukshetra war she disclosed the secrecy prevailed around Karna's birth to the Pandavas and decided to offer liberation and proper homage to Karna, their elder brother. The pain, yet the fortitude of Karna too, get evolved in the play.

When Kunti entered the battlefield, the meaninglessness of human existence was manifested through the long call of the bird and at last she decided to accompany Dhritrashtar and Gandhari to the forests seeking penance. Kunti was always bewildered with the invisible presence of the bird:

> That mysterious, unknown figure…there…it seems I can see it…over there…the woods that look like collyrium beyond the cool blue of the Ganga…and amidst the blue shades there, the wings fluttering…and amidst the rhythm and harmony of cricket's songs, the bird call…something, something that has shocked me, drained me, at every juncture…
> Is it the sign of my heart's desires? Is it the flappings of Lord Agni's wings that I hear? Or the rising rhythm of my heartbeats? (*Wings* 82).

The play ends with Kunti renouncing her worldly bondages and entering into *vanaprastha*. Both the literary texts, *Karan Kunti Samvad* by Tagore and *Wings Flapping Somewhere* by G. Sankara Pillai eloquently portray the character of Kunti which is far different from Vyasa's Kunti. Though she appears to be a strong-willed woman in *Mahabharata*, she too undertakes consecutive episodes of trials, tribulations, anxieties, dilemmas and turmoil in her life regarding the birth of Karna and its aftermath. These conflicts in her motherhood didn't get full expression in our holy *Puranas* and the literary doyens. Tagore and Pillai, perceived Kunti as a human being with her flaws and limitations. A thorough deconstructive reading of *Mahabharata* could be seen in these two literary canons as they unfolded the fissures and gaps in the myths and revealed the bond between the fostered son and a long-lost natural mother in these tales of motherhood.

Works Cited

Barthes, Roland. *Mythologies.* Translated by Annette Lavers. Hill and Wang, 1972.

Hutcheon, Linda. *The Canadian Postmodern: A Study of Contemporary Canadian Fiction.* Toronto UP, 1988.

Johnson, Barbara. *The Cultural Difference: Essays in the Contemporary Rhetoric of Reading.* John Hopkins UP, 1980.

Pillai, G Sankara. "Wings Flapping Somewhere." *Comparative Literature*, edited by Subin Varghese, Macmillan Publishers India Pvt Ltd, 2019, pp 69-83.

Tagore, Rabindranath. "Karna Kunti Samvad." *Comparative Literature*, edited by Subin Varghese, pp 57-66.

Warner, Marina. *Managing Monsters: Six Myths of Our Time.* Vintage, 1994.

Chapter 7

Myths, Women, and Subalternity: An Analysis of Kavita Kane's *Lanka's Princess*

Anshuman

> Within infinite myths lies the eternal truth. Who sees it all?
>
> Varuna has but a thousand eyes, Indra has a hundred, And You and I, only two.
>
> (Pattanaik 9)

I

Myths are primarily known as tales weaved together in a grand narrative style, such as an epic or Purana. Written for the readers with an aim to create moral, social and cultural understanding, myths were carved around stories of selflessness, sacrifice, devotion, dedication and truthfulness. Existing through centuries, myths are passed through generations, thus influencing thoughts and creating changes in one's life and personality. Myths, as old as the sky's existence, serves as morality tales and act as true inspiration for the general populace while becoming a source of writing for many writers and poets in India and abroad. Myth and truth are often conflicted with reference to the truthfulness and falsity of the information provided. Although truth or *satya*, can be understood as complete truth, whereas myths or mythology is weaved around partial truth or references to some true happenings or the perception of the person which itself depends on some truthful evidence. As Pattanaik asserts, "Ancient Hindu seers knew myth as mithya. They distinguished it from '*sat*'. Mithya was truth seen through a frame of reference. '*Sat*' was truth independent of any frame of reference" (16).

Ancient mythology and myths stressed on following the socially accepted moral and righteous path often seemed partial and discriminatory. Heavily loaded with patriarchal notions and misogynistic interpretations, mythology holds innumerable examples of female subjugation and discrimination. The persecutors, often the kings or the men in power, were made to outshine and were gloriously portrayed whereas the victims, the women, were made to suffer and endure. With the revival and awakening, many writers came across outstanding reinterpretations of the existing texts, thus making the most silent characters speak for themselves. Pioneers of mythology and mythopoeia, Devdutt Pattanaik and Kavita Kane have carved a special niche for themselves in the literary world as their portrayal, interpretation and reinterpretation of the texts have made us aware of many silently existing outstanding characters.

Mythopoeia, a term having its roots in the Hellenistic or Biblical Greek word *muthopoila*, means myth-making or constructing myths. First recorded in 1846, the term was used for the narrative genre where fictional or artificial mythology is created with reference to mythical tales, incidents or characters. The meaning came into practice after "Mythopoeia", a poem by John Ronald Reuel Tolkien, gained popularity and currency in literary world. The poem was written in 1931 and published in a collection named *Tree and Leaf*; the poet explained and defended the creative process of myth-making, thus integrating and reinterpreting the mythological themes, archetypes and tales with modern perspectives, and hence, thus creating myths remains the main focus of this genre.

Mythopoeia, a practice allowing reinterpretation of tales, helps to achieve new understandings, as writers often experiment by changing the narrative style, visualising the victims and listening to the silent ones. A reversal or redistribution of hegemonic power, displacing the power structures and retelling the mythic tales from the perspective of marginal ones allows the writer to help the readers interpret and evaluate the two sides of the same coin.

Kavita Kane, a pioneer of Indian mythological fiction and mythopoeia, has tried to shape the ideology of readers by her outstanding creation, for instance, *Lanka's Princess,* a tale of Meenakshi who was labeled Surpanakha, the infamous demonic character accused of creating all chaos. The sister of famous King Ravan, Vibheeshan and Khumbhkarn, Surpanakha was named Meenakshi, the one with beautiful fish-shaped eyes, at birth. Rishi Vishravas, son of Pulastya and the grandson of Brahma, the creator of Universe, was Meenakshi's father who was often perceived as ugly, untamed, brutal and brazen woman. Out rightly rejected and unloved by her mother Kaikesi, Meenakshi was often belittled over her looks and physical appearance. As Kaikesi asserts, "She hardly looks beautiful or like me. In fact she's quite ugly!" (*Lanka's Princess* 2). Enduring several stigmas and accusations, Meenakshi aka Surpanakha was labeled to be the catalyst of a deadly war between Ram and Ravana in most narratives. Mythological references pointed her out for the annihilation of her family and a reason for several deaths. Considered as the evil and mischievous character in the great historical narrative *Ramayana*, Meenakshi aka Surpanakha, the most misunderstood character in *Ramayana*, grew up in the shadows of her brothers who were destined to win wars, fame and prestige whereas she, charted out a path filled with misery and revenge. Enduring criticism and a stigmatised existence throughout, Meenakshi was brought to the fringes of life, thus making her a subaltern who was unloved, rejected, abused and neglected throughout, assigning a subaltern status and dragging her to marginalisation. Kavita Kane's protagonist was not portrayed as a furious and ravenous female demon who raged her brother's anger and fueled the war, rather she is shown as an intelligent, sharp witted, bold and fiery woman yearning love, happiness and acceptance who had often been misinterpreted, misunderstood and mistreated.

II

Subaltern, a term used to define those who are of lower rank or status, was adopted and used by Italian Marxist philosopher, linguist and politician, Antonio Gramsci to refer to the working class in the Soviet Union and who were subjected to the hegemony of the ruling classes. The difference between the struggle of the subaltern classes and those belonging to power structures can be marked by the fact that those belonging to the hegemonic power structures were listened to and recorded in history whereas the struggling class history was not ever accepted as official or real. Thus, Gramsci argued that "the subaltern classes have the same complex history as that of the hegemonic classes, although the latter constitutes the most officially accepted" (Louai 5). Subaltern studies strive to allow the general, unvoiced people to speak within the pages of elitist historiography and attempts to let the victims speak for themselves, thus imparting voice to the unheard oppressed sections. Subaltern studies have pioneers worldwide such as Ranajit Guha, Gayatri Chakravorty

Spivak, David Arnol, Parth Chatterjee, Shahid Amin, Dipesh Chakrabarty and Gyanendra Pandey, who, in one way or the other, have highlighted the marginalised and subjugated classes in history and literature in order to bring them from periphery to the centre.

Subaltern studies, as a concept, gained momentum and popularity after the arrival of the ice-breaking essay, *Can the Subaltern Speak?* written by Gayatri Chakravorty Spivak, cultural-marxist theorist and an Indian-American scholar. Emerging in 1985, the essay is a critical commentary on subalternity that primarily deals with problems related to patriarchal structures and gender issues. Referring to the case of Sati, a historical practice banned by Britishers in India, Spivak portrayed the Sati women as a group of subalterns whose persecutors exist in the same setup. Spivak's whole discourse refers to speaking for the unvoiced, oppressed and suppressed sections of society, which largely includes disempowered women.

The mythological tales that the world read and listen to have always resonated about male supremacy, their grandeur, power and glorification. The relationship of subalternity and mythology is ages old as various anecdotes reflect the powerlessness, degradation and dehumanisation of women. Labeling and portraying women as vamps, faulty and negative characters has always created a binary such as normal and deviant, good and bad, positive and negative. Vulnerable women characters such as Mandodari, Draupadi, Surpanakha, Hidimbi and Menaka are portrayed and defined in terms of subalternity. Women, children, poor, powerless and those with lower castes and classes have always suffered and endured in the hands of persecutors who are often the male members of the society or the bourgeois. The glorification of women in mythology can be interpreted by several goddesses for instance Kali, Durga, Sarasvati or Laxmi. The common relationship these famous names share is of power whereas those who are not provided special powers were always seen below the margins.

Marginalisation, a discrimination in a larger sense, has been a key factor in subalternity. Those carrying a subaltern status are often seen deprived of rights, equal status and voice in the society. Various queens and women of mythology have faced oppression in the hands of society and men especially. Mythological female characters such as Surpanakha, Draupadi, Menaka, and Sita are few names whose roles were interpreted with patriarchal lens and their contributions and roles to their existing setup was never fully admired or justified, thus making them subaltern of the existing society. The marginalisation and subaltern status of these women is not only limited to societal level rather it's more familial and personal. Surpanakha, a bold and brave, character of mythology endured discrimination at familial and societal level, often labeled as demoness and vamp, her persecutors were her own family and associated clan.

III

Princess of Lanka, Meenakshi, an unloved child since the time of birth, was often called ugly and an ogre. The life-long struggle of conflict between beautiful and ugly was hindered much when she was mutilated in the hands of Lakshman. Meenakshi, born to a great Rishi and asura clan endured criticism for her looks and fiery nature. The misogynistic interpretations and the societal standards of beauty have always caused harm to her psyche which became an obstacle for her to accept herself as a beautiful girl. Kaikesi, despite being Meenakshi's mother always saw her with hatred and disgust as she was a barrier in accomplishing Kaikesi's dream of making an asura empire with her sons thus aiming to conquer the three worlds and Lanka. At an unease due to Meenakshi's birth that too with dark complexion, Kaikesi asserts, "How is this dark monkey going to bring us good fortune? No one will ever marry her!" (*Lanka's Princess* 3). Calling her ugly spinster and staring at the baby's abnormally long nails, 'Chandranakha' was the only name she could think of at that time. Meenakshi, a victim of constant discrimination was criticized for her looks and for her arrival as an obstacle in Kaikesi's plan. Kaikesi often reprimanded her daughter, Meenakshi for her witty remarks with derogatory comments and name calling making her recall what society made her realise about her looks. Kaikesi criticized, "The cruel tongue of yours, Surpanakha. You are as hard as your nails!!" (*Lanka's Princess* 128).

In aesthetics and major aspects of life, binary categorisation is prevalent and works having two extremes, creating normal and deviant, good and bad, just and unjust, the two unmatched ends running parallel. The subversive journey of Meenakshi from Chandranakha often involves disapproval by her mother, Kaikesi itself. Although she received love from her father, Vishravas, she feared the often rejection that she received on her mother's behalf as she labeled her a cheater for failing her plans and was more inclined towards her male children as they seemed to be the accomplishers of her dream project of ruling the *asura* kingdom.

Gender discrimination, an under rooted cause of gender based hierarchy, serves as a malfunction in the society. The male supremacy, an ideology striving to belittle and subjugate women, is largely based on misogynistic interpretations, rigid gender roles and patriarchal structures. The placement of masculine viewpoint and male ideology as the center of the world's view and interpreting culture, history and society with those lenses defines Androcentrism, which shows how females are marginalised. Kaikesi's world was in larger sense androcentric as her whole discussion referred to praising and supremacy of her male children, thus often labeling and belittling Meenakshi for being a girl, and creating a less powerful women, "Vibhishan is a boy, and he's older to you. He doesn't need your protection!" (*Lanka's Princess* 5). Meenakshi encountered the gender based discrimination at early stages in her home and in the hands of her mother. A regular victim of her brother's anger, Meenakshi witnessed pain of sacrifice and loneliness from childhood. Merciless strangling of her favorite pet, her lamb named Maya, by her own brother Ravan, left Meenakshi in pain and anguish, forcing her to fight back and leading to tearing, scratching, biting and ultimately owning the label of being, Surpanakha. It was not her acceptance of pain, rather the denial that made her call and named, Surpanakha, "He had rechristened her Surpanakha after that fateful assault and the name had stuck. Everyone teased her with that hateful name and she knew Ravan derived a vicarious glee each time he saw how the name affected her when it was uttered" (*Lanka's Princess* 11).

Perceived as less powerful and the unimportant Other, Meenakshi was made to realise the difference between her brother's power and her powerlessness. Simone De Beauvoir in her seminal work, *The Second Sex* discusses the numerous factors that dictate the conduct of being a woman as per the society's norms which leads to the further subjugation of woman. Simone asserts, "One is not born, but rather becomes, a woman" (14). Kaikesi left no stone unturned to make her daughter realise how she was the 'less other' existing amid powerful clan.

Meenakshi aka Surpanakha, the sole struggling character in the narrative who dares to love and selects her life partner Vidyujiva despite her family's opposition, was left deprived of the love she craved since childhood. Although, her love was real and she married

Vidyujiva who brings out the lovely Meenakshi in her conquering all odds. Continuing to be an ill-fated, unloved and detestable protagonist, she soon became a widow as she discovered that her brother, Ravan had killed her husband. Utterly dedicated to seek revenge, she lashed out at her brother who was the persecutor, according to Meenakshi. She accused the family of being traitors and monsters whereas Khumbhkaran and the rest of the family try to persuade her by claiming that he was innocent. Although righteously introduced with her brother's intention she knew that Ravan has killed her husband as he posed a threat to the throne of asura empire, tormented and struggling, she blamed her brother, "You killed whatever I had. And it is because of only one man-Ravan. Ravan hated him, Ravan dreaded him, Ravan was threatened by him and what does Ravan do to anyone who challenges him?" (*Lanka's Princess* 172).

Surpanakha abandons both her paternal place, Lanka and her identity as Meenakshi after her husband, Vidyujiva's death. Identifying back with her ferocious nature for the purpose of exacting wild justice, vengeance was the only option left with her. As Kane describes, "From henceforth she was Surpanakha: she was shrugging off the cloak of Meenakshi forever as she left the shores of Lanka" (179). Surpanakha, keen to seek revenge, planned to train her son Sambhu Kumar, who will be able to achieve her revenge but fate was again unjust and cruel to her as she was further marginalised and prevented from achieving her ambitions. Surpanakha got distraught when she discovered her only son is dead and his head is lying severed in the wilderness. The widow woman, Meenakshi, now is a mother carrying the pain of death of her only son. Fighting with loneliness, she was visiting past memories and adopted crazy ways to cope up with isolation and pain, "She got up for a brisk walk: another antidote to that sweeping loneliness, a habit she has acquired to kill that darkness smothering her" (*Lanka's Princess* 194).

Blazing in anger and pain, Surpanakha adopted the true meaning of her name and was in frenzy to punish the persecutor but she was further marginalised and humiliated. Her family, love and beauty, everything was at stake, the persecutors of Surpanakha was none other than her family members. The entrance of Ram and Lakshman in Dandak fills her with optimism as her utter belief that she can use them as pawns and her revenge plan would succeed. Although the intervention of cruel faith again hindered her, giving her the worst experience that reshaped her whole life, the mutilation. Surpanakha was mutilated as a result of her desire to copulate with any one of Ram or Lakshman and her jealousy upon witnessing the beautiful queen, Sita and in an attempt to drag her out, she ended up doing her own acute marginalisation. On realising the harm done, Surpanakha was devastated as she, "clutched her hands over her chest, on her knees, begging, sobbing for mercy, the blood and tears dripping off her bowed, mutilated face" (*Lanka's Princess* 203). Panic-stricken princess was left in woods with the bloodied face, crying over her fate as the mutilation was not a harm to her face rather it was an incident of shame and dishonor as she "turned and ran, forcing her feet to flee, in a fire of agony, her fingers splayed over her bloodied face, hoping to cover the pain and the shame" (Kane 203), broken into pieces, Meenakshi was shattered.

The mutilation, an act of severe impairment is not only a removal or amputation of a body's part rather it denotes the reshaping of her whole personality. The mutilation of nose, a principal element, a sensory organ and an important feature of one's beauty can be understood as an aesthetic element which, if done, can cause psychological harm too. Surpanakha keen to fight back was blazing in fire whereas Lakshman defended, "Evil has no gender, lady, and in war too, the enemy has no gender" (*Lanka's Princess* 202). Surpanakha endured humiliation and loneliness throughout her life. Often labeled as cause of Ravan's death, Surpanakha remained faithful to her long-lost land, Lanka as the war again brought bad luck with sweaping off all her brothers including the favorite ones, Kumbha and Meghnad.

Living in much trauma and pain, Surpanakha was throughout cornered, humiliated and discriminated. Despite being born in a powerful clan, she was criticized for being less beautiful, powerful and witty. Deprived of love since childhood, Surpanakha endured isolation and craved for companionship and love. Victim in hands of family and society, she became a homeless widow roaming in bewilderedness carrying the pain of lost Kingdom, dead husband and son. Enduring the stigma, inflicted by her own brother, Surpanakha, once princess Meenakshi, depicts the dehumanising behaviour and insensitive attitude towards women. Often interpreted over her own actions, Surpanakha is labeled as a demoness and succumbs woman of mythology, was called the flag bearer of the great war between Ram and Ravan. The journey from Meenakshi to Surpanakha was full with pain, trauma, loss, humiliation, marginalisation and scarcity of all life pleasures. Deprived of partner's care, child's love, brother's companionship and mother's affection, Meenakshi's journey was that of a subaltern. The so called sultry voluptuous woman, Surpanakha was assigned a name out of anger and conflict, which was often validated at home " her mother always called her by that detestable name when she was particularly displeased with her" (*Lanka's Princess* 88).

The presence of Surpanakha and her description in mythological tales refers to the compromised status of the women and their insensitive treatment by the society driven by patriarchy. The binary oppositions of powerful and powerless, good and bad, beautiful and ugly is present throughout the mythological tale, *Ramayana*, which further describes the subaltern status assigned to Meenakshi as a woman. The deviant other, powerless, bad and ugly, as defined, Meenakshi is an evident example of compromised treatment of women in mythology and denotes the discriminatory gender roles. Construction of gender and the suggestive roles, heavily shaped by culture, society and patriarchy, gender "should be overthrown, eliminated, or rendered fatally ambiguous precisely because it is always a sign of subordination for women" (Butler xiii).

Women's limited voice in the society, patriarchal and social norms often reinforcing the notion of men being more powerful than women, having more prominent voice and position serves to the stereotypical viewpoints of society that was well labelled and validated by mythological tales which are practiced and preached in the society. In mythology and real life, consideration of women as a mere instrument in the hands of societal norms and limiting her to the status of subaltern by her constant subjugation, marginalisation and dehumanisation has the underlying cause, patriarchy, which constantly strangles women in all spheres of life leading to her subordination. In *The Second Sex,* Simone De Beauvoir asserts:

> By the time humankind reaches the stage of writing its mythology and laws, patriarchy is definitively established: it is males who write the codes. It is natural for them to give woman a subordinate situation; one might imagine, however, that they would consider her with the same benevolence as children and animals. But no. Afraid of woman, legislators organise her oppression (114).

Works Cited

Beauvoir, Simone de. *The Second Sex*. Vintage Books, 2011.

Butler, Judith. *Gender Trouble: Feminism and the Subversion of Identity*. Routledge, 1989.

Kane, Kavita. *Lanka's Princess*. Rupa, 2017.

Louai, El Habib. "Retracing the Concept of the Subaltern from Gramsci to Spivak: Historical Developments and New Applications." *African Journal of History and Culture,* vol. 4, no. 1, Jan. 2012, pp. 4–8., doi:10.5897/ajhc11.020.

Pattanaik, Devdutt. *Myth = Mithya: A Handbook of Hindu Mythology*. Penguin, 2008.

Chapter 8

Mythicizing 'the Brahminical Knowledge' through Myth in Girish Karnad's *The Fire and The Rain*

Shobha R

'What is knowledge?'–the question, by which many books on the philosophy of knowledge have begun with, would give an apparent drive to this article, as 'knowledge' is the soul of the discussion in this paper. We must acknowledge that 'economy' and 'knowledge' are the two omni-competent sources which give rise to 'power' and 'dominance' to hold the control over any hierarchical society. The generally accepted definition of knowledge is that it is knowing the justified belief. However, one cannot confine to this definition. As many definitions are possible as many thoughts are. Yet we can understand it on the basis of its functions in the society. I would like to concentrate on three important grounds on which knowledge would be understood, to justify the title of this article.

Firstly 'Knowledge' with the capital 'K' which is not always based on objective facts, has always an exclusion of 'knowledge' with small letter 'k'. In this regard, it is apt to quote the words of Kenneth T. Gallagher – "The existence of knowledge, and the partial transparence of knowledge to itself is an ultimate and irreducible given" (10). Secondly, we cannot be judgmental regarding the assertion 'knowledge is always certain'. This can be better explained with Kenneth's interpretation, "once we cease to think of knowledge as something we either "have" or "do not have", as a static acquisition, many difficulties will appear in a new light. If knowledge is a modality of human existence, then it is subject to the same limitations as that existence; just as man is not what he is, so he does not know what he knows"(14). Thirdly, 'knowledge is not always justified' and at the same time 'it can be nullified'. In this light, Girish Karnad's play *The Fire and the Rain* provides a stage for the discussion on 'the certainty of brahminical knowledge' based on above said aspects. The playwright strategically used a myth to unveil the myth of brahminical knowledge which reigned for many centuries and continued to reign yet, is 'merely a set of unjustified beliefs'.

India is known for its diversity in culture, language, religion, beliefs, etc. Yet 'homogenisation' is an adopted imperial project, a product of British imperialism in India taken by Hindu fundamentalists. 'Homogenisation' is featured with monopolising one God, one religion, one culture and bringing 'oneness in every aspect'. This violent yearning for oneness is a dream in India. Though, Hindu religion broadly includes all the castes and categories of India, inherently it is dominated by brahminical ideology which is expected to be throng in India. It is acknowledged that 'knowledge' was only meant for Brahmins. They stand between Gods and the people as in the words of M. Hiriyanna "as importing of the magical element into Vedic religion …. As a sign of the transfer of power from the gods to the priests" (16). Only literature, especially religious reigned the throne of knowledge. Theatre was an exclusion. The actors were cursed as outcastes by Brahmins. This suppression of drama and acting has severely struck down Karnad. It also led him to write *The Fire and the Rain* to reintroduce and reinstate drama to its position while negating the assumed brahminical knowledge from its prime position.

Girish Karnad, is the unapologetic critic of any extreme 'isms'. He sharply criticizes brahminical ideology, caste system, male sexuality, binary oppositions, cultural domination and asserts the rights of the suppressed 'knowledge', 'men and women' and 'feelings and thoughts'. He revolted against the 'silencing of secular intellectualism' in India. He declared himself 'Me too an Urban Naxal', by hanging a placard around his neck, when he participated in the programme to commemorate the anniversary of Gouri Lankesh's murder. In the play, *The Fire and the Rain,* Karnad directly attacks the authenticity of brahminical knowledge and puts forth the play, the secular performance, as a superior art to Yajna, a sacred performance which is established in the prime position in the hierarchy of knowledge. He uses the myth of Yavakri as a powerful tool to subvert dominance of brahminical knowledge and raises skeptical attitude about its certainty, usage and outcome.

Myth is a narrative in which the characters are usually gods, celestial beings, demi-gods and supernatural elements and agencies. Myth has been interpreted and analysed variously by Roland Barthes in his seminal book *Mythologies*. It seems that Karnad has rightly appropriated the assertion of Barthes that "myth is the most appropriate instrument for the ideological inversion which defines this society" (168). Karnad has tactfully tried this through the myth of Yavakari with however, some modification. He inverted the brahminical ideology which gave rise to the trajectory of knowledge in the web of assumptions, projected as superior and sacred one. He has instilled 'a conjuring trick' (169) in the myth to 'reintroduce society' (131) into it. He has strategically assigned it the task of "historical intention, a natural justification and making contingency appear eternal" (168). Karnad's reading of the play, after its completion, made him to explore the function of the myth. He could be able to trace out "subconscious signals which lead to another myth which in turn will act as a conduit to a third one" (69). As Barthes states, the myth of Yavakari in *The Fire and the Rain* "has turned reality inside out, it has emptied it of history and has filled with nature, it has removed from things their human meaning" (169).

Barthes asserts that "myth is depoliticized speech" (169). We have to reside with Marx to answer the question, is the myth of Yavakari depoliticized or politicized? He said that one cannot find the most natural object with a political trace and the human act produced, fitted up, used, subjected or rejected it (Marx 171). Barthes said that human beings' relationship with myth is based on truth which they depoliticize according to their needs. Karnad had depoliticized the myth of Yavakari to politicize the myth of brahminical knowledge adjoined with the myth of performance. He throws light on the beliefs on brahminical knowledge as god-given and the futility of such knowledge. He also brings forth unrivaled knowledge of theatre which is marginalised.

Karnad came across this peripheral tale in Rajagopalachari's abridgement of *Mahabharata*. In the Myth of Yavakari, Bharadwaja and Raibhya were two friends and sages. Karnad made them brothers in the play. Karnad opined that "it seemed logical that Yavakari should be their cousin though *Mahabharatha* does not explicitly say so" (69). King's decision of selecting of Paravasu, the eldest son of Raibhya, for conducting *yajna*, a fire sacrifice, as a chief priest to bring rain, humiliated Yavakari. So, he went off to the forest for *tapasya* (penenance) to get the knowledge of *vedas* from the gods directly. Here, the assumption about *tapasya* has been unveiled, clearly indicated in the words of Yavakari. In the play, the nomination of Paravasu as a chief priest, has enraged both Yavakari and his own father Raibhya. After this, Yavakari molest Raibhya's daughter-in-law. Incensed Raibhya invokes *kritya* spirit. He conjures a woman who looked like his daughter-in-law and *rakshasa* from his affairs.

In the play, Karnad allowed Raibhya to invite only *Brahma-rakshasa* to kill Yavakari. He weaved a plot about love story between Yavakari and Vishaka, before her marriage and after his return from penance. Another change in the play is that Bharadwaja death is excluded. In the original myth, Bharadwaja dies after the death of her son. Raibhya was killed by Paravasu who mistook him to be a wild animal. But Paravasu kills his father intentionally, as he conjured *Brahma Rakshasa* to create disturbances to *yajna* performance to bring rain. In the original myth, Yavakari, Raibhya and Bharadwaja's lives are restored. But in the play, Indra demotivates Aravasu to deviate from that demand by making him to realise the recycle of the life wheel.

There are also major inclusions in *The Fire and the Rain* by the playwright. Like Shakespeare's *Hamlet,* we can find a technique named 'a play within a play'. In *Hamlet*, a short play is performed in the court to mimic the murder of Hamlet's father. In *The Fire and the Rain*, a performance of the slaying of the demon Vritra by Indra, another myth which is drawn from *Rigveda* is plotted to reveal the nature of Brahminicide. About the inclusion of this plot, Karnad revealed that "Years later, while re-reading the original version, I was astonished to find that right at the beginning of the tale of Yavakari, Lomasha mentions that the whole story took place on the banks of a river in which Indra had bathed to cleanse himself of the sin of killing Vritra" (69). This is plotted to outwit theatre performance over *yajna*, a fire sacrifice.

The creation of the character named Nittilai, a hunter girl; The courtship between Aravasu and Nittilai; Nittilai's interrogation of Yavakari's knowledge and brahminical knowledge; her dying as 'a sacrificial animal' (58); Aravasu love for a hunter girl; his readiness to be expatriated from his caste; his interest in the play, and his sacrifice at the fireplace, forms the heart of the play. It seems that Nittilai and Aravasu are two arms of the playwright and myth is his brain and play itself is his heart. He speaks through her character. His interrogations are placed through her. His anger about the brahminical suppression is expressed through Aravasu. At the end, Aravasu's performance pleases Indra to rain. These are the major modifications, brought out in the play to mythicize the brahminical knowledge which gives 'natural image to an historical reality', as Barthes observes that this naturalisation is the essential function of the myth (169).

Interrogating universalised truths is one of the major agenda of Karnad. *The Fire and the Rain* is not an exception to it. There is a sharp criticism against the terms 'knowledge', 'universal knowledge' and 'brahminical knowledge'. Two types of knowledge have been targeted – knowledge of Yavakari, directly received from God, and knowledge of Raibhya and Paravasu, considered as learned men in the land. Yavakari's gain of knowledge is interrogated by Nittilai and finally nullified by himself. When Nittilai comes to know about Yavakari and Indra's blessings on him by Andakha, she analyses the pathetic condition of the people and what Yavakari could have asked when he met Indra. She narrates that the land was drought stricken; women with babes on their lips, shrunken children, shriveled old men and women gather in front of her house for grains. According to her, if Yavakari would have asked for downpours, his rigorous penance of ten years would have served the purpose. She had two questions: Can he make it rain? Can he tell when he is going to die? It is her assertion that there is no use of knowledge if it can't be used to save dying children and predict one's moment of death.

Nittilai is a staunch critic of 'brahminical knowledge' in the play. Her question "Why are the Brahmins so secretive about everything" (10) digs the way out to sharpen the minds which have been surrendered to 'unrivaled superiority of brahminical knowledge'. She brings out the contrast between their Gods and Hindu Gods. She asserts that "the fire sacrifices are conducted in covered enclosures; they mortify themselves in the dark of the jungle. Even their gods appear so secretly" (10). In contrast, the deity will be invoked in public by the priests on a scheduled day. One can feel the appearance of a spirit to come and go. These words of Nittilai remind us of Kancha Ilaiah's work *Why I am not a Hindu*. Ilaiah has given a brief account of the differences between *brahmin*, *baniya*, as such upper castes and *dalit-bahujans* in gods, cultural practices, beliefs, narratives. Nittilai insists Aravasu not to play the role of Indra as she doesn't like Indra who killed his own brother Vishwarupa.

Yavakari laughs at the very mention of 'universal knowledge' by Vishaka. Yavakari's realisation about the appearance of God clears the cloud. He says: "One would expect the appearance of a god to be a shattering experience. Concrete. Indubitable. Almost physical. But though I think Indra came to me several times, I was never certain" (13). Yavakari's proposition on God's appearance and universal knowledge is based on Rene Descartes' assertion 'I am thinking therefore I exist' (14). He thought that Indra appeared but he was not certain. His penance ended not with success but by his decision. He decided to end and he didn't know what made him to come to such conclusion? Again, he thinks that he has mystical powers that he hadn't before. Yet he was uncertain. Girish Karnad makes it clear that one cannot achieve knowledge through austerities. Indra's words throw light on this. He tells Yavakari "Knowledge is time. It is space. You must move through these dimensions...You can't cross a full stream on a bridge of sand" (13). But Yavakari was adamant. He continued his penance by standing in middle of the fire. Yavakari does not want the 'knowledge' Indra wanted to give. According to Indra, 'Knowledge involves control of passions, serenity, objectivity' (23). That knowledge is suicide for Yavakari. He wanted obsession, hatred and venom. He wanted the knowledge which makes him vicious and destructive. It can be analysed that each person has own understanding of knowledge. Hence, the concept of 'universal knowledge' can be nullified. And another insight is that knowledge can be preservative and destructive. Even though Nittilai is considered learned like Yavakari, Raybhya, Paravasu and Bharadwaja, her knowledge of life, god, and human values is preservative. Yavakari wanted to betray Indra because he felt that he was left ignorant by Indra. After ten years of penance and austerities, Yavakari feels that he is ignorant. Karnad gives another view of knowledge that really was longed by Yavakari and understood by Vishaka. Vishaka finds no difference in Yavakari after penance. Her knowledge about him is that he hasn't yet changed a bit. So she says "I'll give the knowledge Indra couldn't give you, my body – it's light with speech now" (17).

Raibhya, one of the learned sages, was eagerly waiting for the honour to be selected as the chief priest for the seven years of *yajna*, a fire sacrifice, conducted by the king. He was utterly distressed by not being selected. He started hating his own son, Paravasu for being selected as the chief priest. He wanted to avenge Paravasu. He abused his wife Vishaka sexually. He used his knowledge to give birth to *Brahmaraksha* by his hair to kill Yavakari and disturb the fire sacrifice. He expresses his frustration by asserting his power and physical strength – "I shall outlive my sons…long enough to feed their dead souls" (29). He was killed by his own son Paravasu for his vengeance.

Paravasu, the chief priest of the sacrifice, is not either devoted to the sacrifice or to the God Indra. He finds himself equal to Indra. He opines that human beings are defined by their begging. According to him, the fire sacrifice is not sacred one, rather it is a formal rite and structured. It doesn't demand any emotional acrobatics from the participants. If something went wrong in the process, Gods cannot do anything. It has to be set right by a man. He places man superior to God. He is also an unethical man. Though he would be offended of fratricide, he victimizes Aravasu for his crime. Finally, he was paralysed by his own crimes and failed to bring success to the sacrifice. He gets up and without uttering a word calmly walks into the blazing fire.

Karnad provides the detailed note on the myth of the origin of drama in the first chapter of Bharata's *Natyashastra.* It is sandwiched between two performances, neither of which could be described as a success. Rather a misconception about drama is made that it is "precarious, potentially disruptive event" (72). This misconception is inserted because of its social character. Karnad notifies many parallels between *yajna* (sacrifice) and a play. One of the principal differences between the two, as identified by Karnad, is that drama was open to and became the prerogative of castes and communities excluded from *yajna. The Fire and the Rain,* as a whole and 'Indra-Vritra legend' as a 'play within the play' have become instrumental apparatus in the hands of the playwright to interpret the two myths in which the true nature of 'brahminical knowledge' is unveiled which has led to mythicizing brahminical knowledge while creating another myth about a play as a branch of knowledge placed above the *yajna.* Karnad would like to see myth as expressing a deep anxiety that fear of brother destroying brother and Indian obsession with fratricide. He also tries to redefine *yajna* which has been brahminized by quoting the words of Brockington that "sacrifice was a sacrifice of the sacrifice himself and then successively of increasingly remote substitutes (like the horse, the ox, the sheep and then the goat and finally the rice cake)" (72). It seems to be very relevant to redefine history in the contemporary situation in which the whole country is being tried to move against cow-slaughtering. At the end of the original play and play within the play, we find two sacrifices – one is of Paravasu, the representation of evil and Nitilai, the necessary rationale to be instilled in the society. The constructed myth in the play is that it was not the seven years of *yajna* (sacrifice) headed by Paravasu that becomes successful in its purpose but the performance of Aravasu that made Indra to appear and his justly demand which made it rain.

Girish Karnad's *The Fire and the Rain* can be seen as a stage on which many constructive and creative activities have been engineered by its author. Firstly, the myths have been reinterpreted and history has been brought back to its original shape. Secondly, a new perspective of looking at knowledge, especially brahminical knowledge is given. Thirdly, the readers are alarmed to invest their knowledge to understand how myth is presented as a powerful apparatus in the hands of anyone who wants to strongly propagate one's ideology. Last but not the least, the technique of the construction of new myths in order to subvert the domination of any exploitative knowledge is also innovated. Through this play, Karnad has made honest efforts to give a justifiable honour and place to the play, as an art and irrevocably a part of knowledge.

Works Cited

Barthes, Roland. *Mythologies.* Vintage Classics, 2009.

C. Rajagopalachari. *Mahabharatha.* Bharathiya Vidya Bhavan, 1951.

Descartes, René. *Discourse on Method.* Macmillan, 1986.

Ilaiah, Kancha. *Why I am Not a Hindu.* Bhatkel & Sen, 2002.

J.L. Brokington. *The Sacred Thread: A Short History of Hinduism.* Oxford UP, 1992.

Karnad, Girish. *The Fire and the Rain.* Oxford UP, 1998.

Kenneth T. Gallagher. *The Philosophy of Knowledge.* Fordham UP, 1982.

Marx, Karl, et al. *The German Ideology.* Lawrence & Wishart, 1974.

M. Hiriyanna. *The Essentials of Indian Philosophy.* George Allen & Unwin, 1949.

Chapter 9

The Reliable Gods and Goddesses: *A Study of Androgyny, Gender Fluidity and Same-Sex Relationships*

Sandhya Devi N.K and Kirankumar Nittali

Introduction

Ancient texts like *Mahabharata*, *Manusmrithi*, *Krittivasa Ramayana*, *Puranas* and *Kamasutra* have endeavored to categorise heterosexuals, homosexuals, neuters (neither masculine nor feminine) and bisexuals. Even though these texts prefer heterosexuality, there was tolerance for non-heterosexuals. Variants of gender, gender fluidity, miraculous births, merging of sexes, which was once prevalent in ancient India, the intervention of British rule has dismantled those beliefs that were all-embracing and divine. Colonial India criminalised same-sex relations which further brought unprecedented changes in the attitudes of gender roles, gender attitudes, and sexuality which left a fragmented rigid India.

To understand this, first it is important to examine Judith Butler's notions regarding Heteronormativity. The gender norms created by the dominant patriarchy slowly roots itself in the society and hence become normalised or "natural sort of a being" (75). On the same note, patriarchal society encompasses men to do whatever they want and women to conform to the submissive image. Therefore, patriarchy frames models based on the submissive roles of women Issues of homosexuality and sexual minorities are part of this minority group (Warner 6). Using Michel Foucault's theory of power, Butler identifies power structures as the large scale patriarchal system, and she further examines this to conclude how the power relations/structures make patriarchy into a full-fledged concept. Patriarchy is also gender limiting (Butler 125). Due to this, the division is already created and hence inside the society, individuals are forced to assume the given/standardised gender. This results in a clear-cut binary division. Thus, masculinity can be easily differentiated from the feminine and vice-a-versa. And so, femininity cannot exist without masculinity (since masculinity is superior) and hence this binary differentiation is thus absorbed by society through major concepts such as desire, sex, and gender. Yet the author further demonstrates fantasy and the compulsive behaviour that heteronormativity demands and naturalises. The author further speaks on homosexuality that the "construction of coherence conceals the gender discontinuities that run rampant within heterosexual, bisexual, and gay and lesbian contexts" elucidates on how gender norms hold against homosexuality and are in the interests of heterosexuality (Butler 194). This controls the gender identities and weaves a uniform structure for the society to follow the prescribed gender. "Regulatory ideal is then exposed as a norm and a fiction that disguises itself as a developmental law regulating the sexual field" which helps realise that gender is but a fiction and hence an illusion made for the sake of the male-dominated society. Thus it is implied that "neither true nor false but are only produced as the truth" (Butler 200). This is precisely what is taken up in this paper by bringing in the references from a myth to display how gender may not restrict itself in terms of male and female but accept various forms for an all-inclusive society.

Sexuality is numerous and diverse. Yet society believes heterosexuality to be righteous and sacred. The gender that we know and normalise is the gender binary opposition: male and female. Is there space for more? Are there representations of androgyny, gender fluidity and same-sex relationships in Hindu mythology? If so, can it help for an all-inclusive society? The present paper will examine extracts from Hindu Lore and Devdutt Pattanaik's *Shikandi: And Other Tales They Don't Tell You* to understand how concepts of sexuality, gender roles, gender fluidity and androgyny is dealt with. This study tries to showcase reliable myths and stories for validation to sexual minorities and the society to build an all-inclusive society.

Androgyny

Androgyny in its broadest sense is "the One which contains the Two; namely the male (andro) and the female (gyne)" (Singer 20). Androgyny can also be understood as "simultaneously male and female in a physical form" (O'Flaherty 283). Androgyny may have two different forms (O'Flaherty 283). The body is divided into two parts and can have female parts in the first half and male parts in the second half or vice-a-versa. And the second part is divided vertically with half female (usually on the left) and the right half being male. She further goes on to explain Androgyny as one of the ancient prototypes which were found in many myths and lore. Androgyny also symbolises a powerful religious symbol (O'Flaherty 284).

In Hindu mythology, *Ardhanarishwara/Ardhanari* is the linked form of Lord Shiva and Goddess Parvati, or Shakti, is an example of Androgyny. There are many versions of *Ardhanarishwara*. First, as Lord Shiva accepts Ganga, a jealous Parvati asks Shiva to merge with Parvati. The second version of this androgyny is the culmination of Shakti (symbolising power/primordial energy) and Shiva (symbolising the mind) and the third version is Kundalini's (an avatar of Shakti/Parvati) fused form with Lord Shiva. The first and second versions describe oneness and the equal prominence of both the genders. The third describes the union of Kundalini (cosmic energy) and Lord Shiva. Here, the self is freed from the flesh to achieve Samadhi. This state is called supreme consciousness. Another androgynous form of Shiva and Shakti is *Prakriti*[1] (female form)-*Purusha*[2] (male form). Ardhanari-Ganesh mentioned in *Halayudh Stotra* (dates to11th century), Radha-Krishna mentioned in *Puranas* and *Brahmavaivartha* are some androgynous forms.

In different parts of India, both the gods and goddesses in one form are worshipped together. These deities help us realise that androgyny being one of the oldest forms, is second to the Absolute[3]. Many mythologies suggest the primordial deities have both male and female features (Singer 32). This implies that the unified body comes first and subsequently the separated bodies of male and female. Oneness/androgyny is given more importance than separateness.

The Earth deity (female) and Sky deity lay in an everlasting embrace is an example of androgyny from Greek myth. Inari-Okami a Japanese god/kami has male, female and androgynous forms and can take the gender s/he chooses. Examples of Egyptian god Aton, Ptah, Mut, Neith, Greek Gaia, and Roman Jupiter, to further explain

---

1 Prakriti denotes cosmic/creative energy

2 Purusha denotes conscious

3 Absolute refers to the Supreme Being or the Supreme God

Androgyny, are given by (Klonkowska 120). Many cultures, including contemporary Indian culture, fail to acknowledge androgyny due to the threat it causes against male dominance. It also threatens the largely invested gender identities and sex. Therefore, androgyny promotes fluid behaviour and helps to be a tolerant individual. India, with such vast androgynous deities, would it be difficult to accept the non-patriarchal–submissive mode of androgyny? Could incompleteness be reworked to feel wholeness again? It also comes under the realisation that androgynes being primordial and powerful deities disrupt the entire system of the gender binary and the age-old hierarchical ideologies.

Gender Fluidity

Gender Fluidity is defined as "an umbrella term to describe possibilities for gender identity beyond the binary man and woman" (Parkar 165-166). Gender Fluidity may also be understood as deconstructing gender binarism. Mythologies, offer a "suspension of male-female binary oppositions" (Klonkowska 120). The same is explored in Hindu mythology:

> It must be understood that in Sanskrit, grammatical gender is not always a sign of physical sex. Gender infers function, sex infers form; so that an individual may be masculine from one point of view and feminine from another. For example, Prajapati[4] (the Progenitor, m.) can be referred to as "pregnant," Mitra[5] "inseminates Varuna," Brahman (n.) can be regarded as the "womb" of life" (Coomaraswamy 123).

In Hindu myths and stories deities, demigods, and humans either cross their gender boundaries/roles, or there is a sex change. These fluctuations question the rigidity of Gender and disassemble all that is known and believed.

Gender is the social and cultural distinction between male and female and all erotically important aspects of social life and social being, such as impulses, behaviours, relationships, and personalities, are referred to as "sexuality" (Jackson 3-5). He also says, since, what is sexual (erotic) is not set but depends on and varies contextually and historically, this concept assumes fluidity. As a result, there are no direct lines between what is sexual to one person in one context and what is sexual to another person in another context.

---

4 Prajapathi is Lord of creation

5 Mitra is a deity mentioned in Rigveda

The deity Hari-Hara, also known as Shankaranarayana is a fused form of lord Vishnu (Hari) and Lord Shiva (Hara). This linked form depicts gender ambiguity. In another mythical form of Hari-Hara, Lord Shiva merges with Mohini (an avatar of Vishnu). Here Vishnu (male) as Mohini (female) is vivacious, beautiful, and graceful. Lord Vishnu has taken the form of a woman and is womanly. Gender is fluid, and gender roles are reversed. In another myth, Lord Vishnu plays the role of mother to Ayyappa, a progeny of Shiva and Vishnu. As seen here, gender identification becomes troublesome and vague. But the world of gods did not restrict itself to a particular gender or sexuality. A wide range of attitudes and behaviours existed and is undeniable. Hence, sexual and gender boundaries are crossed back and forth. It is also important to note that not everything was about sexuality or sexual in nature and gods and goddess were required to take numerous forms or avatars to uphold *dharma.*

Tamil Bhakti tradition brings forward a story of gender transformation. In this story, Shiva changes into a female form to deliver his devotee. Further, Shiva sings songs to calm the woman in labour, holds her hand and wipes sweat. Shiva's behaviour and body language describe the etiquettes such as soothing, caring and singing all of which are considered feminine (Pattanaik, 2014).

However, it may be worthwhile to realise the breakdown of the male archetypes in mythology and question the contemporary version of Vishnu which has left out Vishnu as a householder, or the nose ring and braided hair that describes Lord Krishna. Were these stories a threat that had been concealed? Would it cause menace in the patriarchal society? "Traditional sex role theories advance that the healthiest, most socially competent orientation for an individual is the one that is consistent with her/his biological sex" says (Elton 292). And yet the strict norm of masculinity is shattered to womanly gaits and traits through these myths and stories. Even though the concept of fixed binary identity is disrupted, gender comfort is implied.

In the Hindu religion, ritual or "*yajna*" plays a major role. Sometimes sages perform rituals and austerities to help infertile couples procreate. This story is extracted from *Mahabharata.* Yuvanashva, of the Ikshvaku[6] clan, asks sages for a solution for infertility, a pitcher of magical water is given to the wives to drink.

---

6 Ikshvaku clan mentioned above refers Ikshvaku dynasty(Sooryavamsa) founded by King Ikshvaku

mistakenly, a tired Yuvanashva drinks this magical water. In time he becomes pregnant, and the baby is surgically removed and delivered. This kind of birth is called "a-yoni-ja" which means 'not born of a womb'. Even though the societal perception of a woman is child-bearer, this story implies the socially and culturally constructed gender can be deconstructed. And it infers that the biological elements that determine gender attitudes may be challenged and revoked.

The story of Bhangashvana from *Mahabharata* discusses the issues of sexuality and gender roles. Bhangashvana bears a hundred children after performing '*yajnas*' but he forgets to mention Lord Indra (Lord of the gods) during the ritual. Indra curses Bhangashvana to change into a woman. She (Bhangashvana) bears a hundred children again. Indra jealous of Bhangashvana's happiness curses the children to kill each other. Bhangashvana appeases Indra. A satisfied Indra asks Bhangashvana two questions. Firstly, to choose between the children who call him mother or father and second, to remain a woman or change back to a man. Bhangashvana chooses the former and decides to remain a woman. This case determines gender fluidity. Gender "fluidity frequently bespeaks uninhibited or potential movement within the space between dualistic categories that substantiate opposing poles. An easy flow between masculinity and femininity, perhaps as recognition of overlapping traits, of potential simultaneous embodiment – these are experiences and concepts often mobilised under the term 'fluidity' (Rehn 461).

Mawu-Lisa of Dahomey mythology has many gender variations. Some sources say that Mawu-Liza's form has one body and two heads. Goddess Mawu Liza also plays different gender roles of son, husband, and messenger. Many such stories insinuate how gender identity and roles easily flow without much adherence to gender binaries. These also represent the opposite of what heteronormativity dictates.

Same-Sex Love/Relationships

In Hinduism, Karmic faiths follow the doctrine of diversity i.e. everyone is different and unique, but the society is ever-changing (Pattanaik 26). Desire being one of the key factors, encourage one to enjoy various sensations and feelings but never without restraint. In Hindu mythology, glimpses into male-male friendship and female-female friendship are constantly seen. *Sushrutha Samhita* from 600 BC,

Caraka Sambita from 200 BC and *Kamasutra* from the 6th century provide details of impotent men – kliba, transgenders – Shanda and homosexuals – asekya. *Kamasutra* is generous in dealing with desire and many references to homosexuality. It defines homosexuals with a term called '*Tritiya-Prakriti*' (third sex or third nature). *Kamasutra* discusses same-sex marriages based on "great attachment and complete faith in one other" (Pattanaik 26). Vedic society included homosexuals as citizens of ancient India who were not subjected to institutions of marriage or procreation. Lesbians could be independent and take jobs (Wilhelm 18). As they were part of the society, they were a part of the literature too. But it is important to note that in the stories, relationships were platonic, romantic, or sexual in nature.

Myths repeatedly describe the close relationship of Shiva and Vishnu through the quote 'Sivasya hridayam vishnur-vishnoschahridayamsivah' – Vishnu is the heart of Shiva and likewise, Shiva is the heart of Vishnu. Another spiritual aspect of Shiva and Vishnu's bonding may be defined as Homosociality[7] and reading through queer eyes makes it difficult to comprehend. He further explains that linking of two gods results in a third god which does not imply that one god has been absorbed into another, nor does it imply that the two deities are identical or that they are moving toward monotheism. Even though these gods represent sustaining masculinity, the existing same-sex bonds blur the lines between homosexuality (strictly non-sexual) and homosociality.

From *Skanda Purana*, the story of Ratnavali contains homoerotic notions. In this story, Ratnavali, the daughter of king Anartha, and Brahmani, the daughter of the king's priest, were best friends and were worried about their separation due to marriage. The king, realising this close relationship, asked King Brihadbala to marry his daughter and the king's priest to marry Brahmani. But due to some reasons, King Brihadbala disagrees to marry Ratnavali. After this, Brahmani refuses to marry the King's priest. The two unmarried girls go to the forest and take refuge near a water tank and perform penance there. Shiva appears to bless Brahmani but again, Brahmani refuses to accept blessings until Shiva blesses Ratnavali. The place

7 Homosociality: Nils Hammarén1 and Thomas Johansson, 2014, defines and describes homosociality "as the social bonds between the persons of same sex men

where both the girls were blessed came to be known as Shudri-Brahmanitirta. This story embodies emotional commitment and seems almost marriage-like. The blessing of Shiva and the awareness of the fathers, acknowledge the existence of same-sex relationships and the inclusive mindset of the society.

The story of Bhagirath from Bengali *Rampanchali* of Krittavasa is another example of same-sex love. King Dilip could not father children even though he had two wives. He begged the sages who prepared a magical potion. Before Dilip could drink it, he passed away. The sages asked one of the wives to drink it and after drinking the potion approach the other wife like a man. Thus, Bhagirath was born from the union of two mothers. The name Bhagirath means born out of two vulvas or *bhagas*. Same-sex love between two women is illustrated.

The story of Samavan and Sumed is of two brahmins who could not get wives due to their poverty. They found out about Simantini, a queen who parted with endowments to one brahmin couple each Monday in the wake of venerating them as Shiva and Shakti. The gifts were necessary for marriage, however, they would not get the gifts without a bride. Samavan disguises himself as a woman and visits Simantini as Sumedhas' wife. Simantini, who perceived this, transforms Samavan into a woman who later is married to Sumed has. Does this imply sex change? Definitely. But even though this is heterosexual marriage, can the fact that Samavan was once a man be erased? Gender variance and same-sex love leanings are blurred. Sexuality itself is blurred. Were these relationships platonic or sexual? Again, it's very difficult to categorise as the situation and time were different. The third sex or nature has various definitions and categories which makes it difficult to use one term. But same-sex love being prevalent was not mainstream. Even if it was mainstream, it was later blurred and faded into the past like a wisp of smoke.

Conclusion

Art, architecture and writings of Ancient India describes the various forms of eroticism. Some of the oldest texts in the world like *Mahabharata* and *Ramayana* represent homosexuality and acknowledge the existence of the third gender. Around 500 BC Buddhism unfolds and *Vedic* culture waned. Yet again during 300 BC Shankaracharya and Ramanuja brought back *Vedic* culture. *Kamasutra* was written. Muslim invasion took place but there was peaceful coexistence for a while. But as Mughal Empire entered India, peace died. Women were mistreated and homosexuals were punished. Mughal Empire subsided and finally in 1757, British East India became dominant in India. Anti-sodomy law which was enforced later becomes section 377 of the Indian Penal Code which criminalises carnal relations that is out of the natural order. Unfortunately, the native Indian culture and traditions were forgotten, and India took a step back from its diversity. Even though in the year 2018, the Antisodomy laws were repealed, the strain that was made remains.

Sexuality, spirituality, and religion are inter-connected. *Kamasutra* explains that desire is not just for reproductive purposes but also to achieve pleasure. Restrain was expected and the dangers of sex were noted but the pleasure was not prohibited or looked down upon in ancient India. Devotion, rituals, sexuality were closely related to each other even though in the contemporary aspect, the concept of non-heteronormative sex or non-marital sex is classified as deviant. *Ramayana*, one of the oldest texts, describes how Lord Rama accepted homosexuals, cross-dressers and transexuals. If we understood that "Vikritievam Prakriti" which means what is unnatural is also natural; the pain and suffering of the sexual minorities may be diminished. Furthermore, the stories on gender fluidity and same-sex relations should emphasise that history be remembered and re-learnt what was once true and inclusive.

It is understood by disrupting gender binaries. Self-identification within prescribed gender categories turns out to be easy and not restricted. Here, the subverted do not have to be subverted in the realm of gods and goddessess. All these representations can refuse and rupture the patriarchal system and reconfigure belief systems. These selected extracts debunk the fixed gender identities formulated by the social and political structures and allow for an all-inclusive society. Gods and Goddesses are reliable, and myths may not stay myths.

Works Cited

Ballard-Reisch, Deborah, and Mary Elton. "Gender Orientation and the Bem Sex Role Inventory: A Psychological Construct Revisited." *Sex Roles,* vol. 27, no. 5/6, 1992, pp 291-306.

Butler, J. *Gender Trouble.* Routledge, 1990.

Coomaraswamy, D. A. "Myths and Symbols in Indian Art and Civilisation." Heinrich Zimmer, *Myths and Symbols in Indian Art and Civilisation*, edited by Joseph Campbell, Pantheon Books,1972, pp 123.

Jackson, S. *Gender, Sexuality and Heterosexuality: The Complexity (and Limits) of Heteronormativity*. Sage Publications, 2006.

Klonkowska, A. M. *Dual-Unity or Dichotomy: Androgyny and Social Construction of Gender Bipartition.* Taylor and Francis Online, 2014.

Mulvey, L. "Visual Pleasure and Narrative Cinema."*Visual and Other Pleasures: Language, Discourse, Society,* edited by Palgrave Macmillan, 1989.

O' Flaherty, W. D. *Women, Andrgynes and Other Mythical Beasts.* The U of Chicago P, 1980.

Parkar, S. *Gender Fluidity–A Spectrum of Identities.* Palgrave Macmillan, 2016.

Pattanaik, D. Introduction. J. Johnson, *I Am Divine So Are You: How Buddhism, Jainism, Sikhism and Hinduism Affirm the Dignities of Queer Identities and Sexualities.* HarperCollins India, 2017.

---. *Shikandi: And Other Tales They Don't Tell You.* Zubaan and Penguin Groups, 2014.

Sedgwick, E. K. *Epistemology of the Closet.* U of California P, 1991.

Singer, J. *Androgyny: Toward a New Theory of Sexuality.* Anchor Press, 1976.

Warner, Michael. "Introduction: Fear of a Queer Planet". *Social Text,* no. 29, 1991, pp. 3-17. JSTOR, www.jstor.org/stable/466295.

Chapter 10

Queerness in Select Stories of Devdutt Pattanaik's *Shikhandi: And Other Tales They Don't Tell You*

Radhika

India is the land of civilisation having various religions, dialects, traditions and cultures. It is a depository of *Puranas*, *Vedas* and famous epics like *Ramayana* and *Mahabharata*. It has a very long cultural history and its literature has its extraction from various *Vedas*, *Puranas* and the epics. These texts talk about the mythological tales that are entrenched in Indian consciousness. These tales and legends help us to move back to the unremembered culture, traditions and beliefs which make it apparent that culture is highly influenced by mythologies.

The interpretation of these mythological stories is firmly affected by the beliefs of the interpreter as well as those of the receiver. This re-interpretation and de-mythification helps to understand myths from a new perspective. Revisioning of the myths is considered as the confluence of mythology and fiction. In the present era, a number of prolific writers like Devdutt Pattanaik, Amish Trpathi, Kavita Kane, Amit Majmudar, to name a few, have given a new dimension to Indian mythological stories by blending these stories with their imagination. Devdutt Pattanaik, in one of his interviews, quoted, "One must distinguish between mythological fiction and mythology. Mythological fiction is very popular as it is fantasy rooted in familiar traditional tales. Mythology itself is about figuring out worldviews of cultures – how people think in a culture" (Pattanaik).

Devdutt Pattanaik is one of the revisionist mythmakers who focus on the relevance of mythology in the present society. He is eminent for taking in the epics like *Ramayana* and *Mahabharata* in human resource management. He views that myth contributes in the development of the society. His perspectives on myths, mythological stories and politics and on sexuality are analytic, creative, ingenious and inspiring. He says that "Hindu mythology focuses on how we see the world; what is seen and unseen and why some things are seen and others unseen" (*Shikhandi* 30). He is the first writer to accept, assemble and remark on the queer ideas in Indian mythological stories. Through his work *Shikhandi: And Other Queer Tales They Don't Tell You*, he compares the queerness in the past with the present. In these tales, Pattanaik touches various topics such as individualism, patriarchy, feminism and gender neutrality. He argues:

> Humanity's discoveries and innovations are shared by history, signs and practices over centuries. These are linked to both the conscious mind and the subconscious mind. The study of the stories, symbols and tradition is mythology. Religion is formed as certain stories and practices become static and are followed by a body that demands access to divine authority. (*Shikhandi* 9)

In modern era, Queer Theory is scrutinised as a branch of Post-Structuralism that emerged in the late twentieth century which incorporates the queer reading of texts and the generalisation of "queerness". Queer Theory points out that gender is a part of essential self, constructed nature of sexual acts and identities. In *Queer Theory: An Introduction*, Annamarie Jagoses focuses on the mismatches between sex, gender and desire which prominently associates with lesbian, Gay, bisexual and transgender (LGBT). Unknown to many, queer is in association with more than 'LGBT' like Cross-dressing, inter-sex, hermaphrodites, gender ambiguity and gender – corrective surgery" (*Queer Theory* 56).

According to Vedantic texts, there are three categories in which human beings are divided according to their sex like 'Purusha' which means male, 'Prakriti' which is females and the last category is ' Tritiya Prakriti' which is for the third gender. Pattanaik points out that "Hindu mythology makes constant references to queerness, the idea that questions notions of maleness and femaleness" (*Shikhandi* 12).

Pattanaik's *Shikhandi: And Other Queer Tales They Don't Tell You* is a collection of numerous Indian myths dealing with the themes like lesbianism, gay, bisexual, transgender and cross-dressing and explores the grim reality of present society. Pattanaik uplifts these issues by focusing on the hidden mythological characters in the grand narratives of Hindu epics. Through the story of Ratnavalli, he explores lesbianism; gay concept is explained in Somavan and Aravan stories; the idea of bisexuality is narrate through the story of Mohini; transgender is described in Arjuna and Shikhandi; the notion of cross-dressing is traced in the stories of Krishna and Samba. Through these tales, Pattanaik brings the concept of queerness, when he says that the "celebration of queer ideas in Hindu stories, symbols and rituals is in stark contrast to the ignorance and rigidity that we see in Indian society" (*Shikhandi* 27).

Mahabharata is the greatest epic of India. The character of Shikhandi plays an important role in *Mahabharata* because his appearance marks a twist in the Kurukshetra War. The story of Shikhandi begins when she borrows the manhood of Sthuna for one night. With this act she proves her masculinity to the princess. This deed of lending made the king Kubera very angry but on the other hand Kubera appreciates the honesty of Shikhandi when she came to Sthuna to return his "borrowed organ" and avows her to use the manhood until her last breath. During the Kurukshetra war, Bhishma confessed his troth of celibacy and that he is the only one to choose the time for his death and no one can kill him. Krishna gave the clue to lower Bhishma's bow before woman and not in front of a man. But as per the law, women were not allowed to enter the battlefield. It was this point of time when Durupada sent his child Shikhandi in front of Bhishma as she was born as a woman but later became a man. Bhishma saw Shikhandi as a woman and lowered his bow and was defeated. In *The Mahabharata: Text as Constituted in its Critical Edition*, Bhishma says:

> This is how, o best of the Kurus, Shikhandin, the excellent charioteer, the son of Durupada, was born as a woman-man. O bull of the Bharatas, the eldest daughter of the king of Kashi, who was well known as Amba, was born in Durupada's family as Shikhandi. If he approaches me, armed with the bow, to fight, I will not look at him for a moment, nor hit him. O joy of the Kurus, I will not use my arrows against a woman, one who was once a woman, one whose name is like a woman's, or one who resembles a woman. For this reason, I will not kill Shikhandi. (59)

This borrowing of the manhood, in the modern times is known as "organ transplantation", in which the transgender prefer medical surgery to change their sexual or gender identity. It helps them to opt their sex as an individual freedom.

The text also deals with gender neutrality by focusing on the portrayals of leading patrons like lord Shiva, Vishnu and Krishna. The role of Krishna flattering himself as a woman is usual in *Puranas*. The mythological stories of Krishna are full of cross-dressing. In the portrayals of Krishna, he is usually seen as wearing a nose ring and also a braided pigtail, which shows that he is comfortable with the feminine attire.

The other story in the collection is about 'Asura' Bhasma who once pleased lord Shiva through his penance to get a boon which gave him power that on whosoever head he would keep his hand would burn into ashes. Taking the advantage of the boon, he tried to lay a hand on everyone and in fact decided to use his power on lord Shiva. Seeing this Shiva went to lord Vishnu to seek his help. Vishnu disguised himself as Mohini, a beautiful woman and went in front of Bhasma. Looking at such a beauty Bhasma decided to marry Mohini. At this point Mohini put a condition that she would only marry him if he dances like her to which he agrees. While dancing Mohini kept her hand on her head and Bhasma did the same which turned him into ashes. Here Vishnu turns himself into Mohini to save Shiva.

There are two other contrasting stories, one of Madurai and the other is of Chidambaram. Once, Madurai was ruled by Meenakshi, three – breasted woman, who wanted to triumph over the world but fell in love with lord Shiva and lost her extra breast. But she remained renowned in Madurai and was worshipped. In the temples, Meenakshi's sculpture is seen as wearing trousers, holding a parrot like peacock and a hanging dragger around her hips. This tales shows a masculine quality of a woman.

In Chidambaram, Lord Shiva is seen as having feminine eminence of dancing and therefore is worshipped as Natraj, God of dance. These narratives show that an individual have both the masculine and feminine quality in them. These stories focus on how God used to change their form from male to female for their devotees. These queer stories are not about sexuality but about the testing notions of gender.

Queerness is well thought-out to be a sexual taboo in Indian traditions. Indian society had a clear concept of masculinity and feminity. The masculine quality requires enthusiasm, courage, knowledge and understanding whereas feminine part includes love, sensitivity, tolerance and commitment. Earlier, all those who were not fit into this domain were excluded and neglected from the society. But now they have been identified as the third gender including 'LGBT' which was legally declared as the third sex by Supreme Court in April 2014.

Work Cited

Jagose, Annamarie. *Queer Theory: An Introduction.* Melbourne U Publishing, 2013.

Pattanaik, Devdutt. *Shikhandi: And Other Queer Tales They Don't Tell You.* Penguin Books Limited, 2014.

---. *Mythological Fiction and Mythology are Different.* Interview by IANS. *The Indian Express*, 10 August, 2017. https://indianexpress.com/article/lifestyle/books/hmythological-fiction-and-mythology-are-different-devdutt-pattanaik.

Udyoga, Parvans. *The Mahabharata: Text as Constituted in its Critical Edition.* Generic, 1984.

Chapter 11

Myth and Retelling of Political Ideologies

R. Umamaheswari

Myth acts as a device in politics to form a disciplined society but stacking in false deceptions to reality for the sake of acceptance is questionable. The idea of Henry Tudor that myth is believed to be true even if it is false is quite negotiable. Debating the aforesaid statements of how myth is interpreted and effectively function in society has resulted only in arguments finding answers. Barthes defines myth as a synonym of ideology in his book *Mythologies*. It is necessary for the world to understand the necessity to drive the weeds of misinterpretations to stand powerfully against the opposition for it requires a trial and error approach.

Myth organises the structure of the social system. Myths and ideologies are ingrained and entrenched firmly in the society. All folktales from history hail from spiritual and religious beliefs of indigenous people and their literature that has great concern over mythology. Roland Barthes talks about myth in *Mythologies* and suggests that it as a second order semiological system. His idea seems to investigate myth and narrative as inseparable concepts and signs. We understand that signs, which appear neutral, are apparently the best vehicle for Ideologies. Everything can turn to be a myth if it is communicated with discourse.

Greek, Rome, Celtic's folktales and oral tradition are connected to their in-built belief system that was nearly turned to ideologies. Hidden scientific truth and unexplained superstition platted behind all rituals narrated in tale form explains the want for a disciplined family or a system. Affective generations of this millennium, longing for transparency, are blind enough to see through the meaning clinging to myth today when their ninety year old granny limits them purposely to a nonsensical truth.

The contemporary western policies formulated now by the westerns were an influence of the Greek and Rome's democratic rule (KRATOS and DEMOS), the judicial system, their people-centered, self-governed and a well-formulated political structure and political ideologies. The Greek god Themis, the Lady of Justice is an inspiration for righteousness and justice is seen as a symbol that is erected in the courthouse of Canada, Ottawa and Tennessee, US is a personification of Greek myth, a symbol of law and representation of myth. Existence of these idols, sculptures and their supernatural powers are unbelievable. The statue of Dike, the daughter of Themis & Zeus, the goddess of Human laws & rights erected in Vermont State today is a symbol of justice, an imaginary sign imported from Greeks. The above references prove that the source of political ideologies is a credit from myth. It's evident that these sets of beliefs exist to discipline the subjects.

Mythology took over literature in 700 BC and developed thereafter. Myth originates in the expression of an experience and the ideologies form the expression of an experience. Echoing the culture and tradition of the ancient, Homer's *Iliad* and *Odyssey* narrate heroism and conquest that models the leadership. *Achilles*' strength, bravery, militancy, honour were significantly a possession of an ideal traitor.

To review the early education system, Gurukul's doctrines and beliefs that had great impact on their students rather than with free will had restricted behaviours under discipline. The progressive world that exists under free will and liberation acquires excess knowledge that has resulted in free living with or without the consideration of family, a hazardous behaviour for a loss of cultural identity and tradition.

Politicalphilosophy anarchism aims to have a rule without a ruler or government. The sub-division, Anarcha-Feminism, a movement for women's emancipation is a reincarnation from Anarchism and Feminism. It is the idea to create equal ground between genders leaving way for liberation and independence without meddling with other social affairs or groups.

Essentially to attain equal freedom in a male dominant society and to empower women is the reality behind this ideology which is misinterpreted by the second generation supporting independable life than equality giving way for conflicts within the same gender. Loss of feminine identity replacing men's role is really a hindrance to the community. Feminist qualities had only overlooked masculinity leading authoritativeness in political and social domain.

Anarcha-Feminism opposed the traditional family education concept discriminating against the roles of gender and disregarded the institution of marriage that entered into coercive contracts. Fear dominated desires and so the social revolution branched out. Emma Goldman, the political activist and anarchist reiterated the need for unhampered growth out of old traditions and habits. The sense of idea of free woman and free love is advocated by Emma Goldman to remove the clutters of hesitation from the minds of women.

Fictional characters like Antigone created by Sophocles could have influenced literature and the world but with irrelevant set of attitudes in today's world, for the world and the society has changed. Loyal reprimands like desecration of corpse does not exist but choosing noble death over a dishonoured life is sensitive and a sensational act but it teaches the world, the importance of values for honour and self-respect.

Existentialism is one similar ideology loaded with liberty that had impressed the teens and was proved scandalous when it has been messed with tradition and culture leaving them to take back seats. Simone de Beauvoir and Sartre, the existentialists chose to live by honesty and of free choice which may not be a right choice for others. The book *The Second Sex* by Beauvoir was a spark for the women to shed their inhibitions taking direct control of their life and many on reading decided to leave their cocoon for a revolution. Beauvoir has stated the way how women grow up less inclined pursuing their goals, self-hesitant, self-doubting than men. The book is a thought of a self-reliant woman. Experimenting or incorporating completely is one's own choice and right.

Existentialism emphasises that human existence has no inherent purpose or meaning where values and meanings are self-created. The strong belief created by myths about life after death in heaven and hell is explained in *No Exit.* Published in 1944 by Jean Paul Sartre, the play makes the audience realise that hell is devoid of tortures and it is mere internal struggles within men that had twisted them with their dishonored desires, uncompromised sins and unpleasant memories.

Waiting for Godot by Samuel Beckett is another similar example of existentialism questioning death and the purpose of human existence with comedy and pathos. *The Myth of Sisyphus* by Albert Camus is a clarity towards human suffering proving it to be meaningless. The theory of absurdity is detailed by Camus. He creates optimism amidst hopelessness to fight the epidemic questioning moral concepts.

Ideology can be the best only if it helps to achieve life-goals not delimiting or humiliating ourselves and the society with certain limitations on the sect of *dharma.*

Transhumanism is another set of ideologies taking technology to the next level adding new life space for beings constructed on the base of advocating the limitations and ethics of using emerging technologies to enhance longevity, mood and cognitive abilities. Transhumanists in the past were great magicians transferring souls to bodies proving human existence in a superficial way. Transhumanists now take technology to a different experience researching to protect humanity against risks like bio and nuclear war or an asteroid collision. Transhumanism believes that humans are capable of transforming themselves with their abilities expanding the situation labeling them as posthuman beings. Machine world was once a myth but society cannot deny the fact that the myth trails the ideology.

Vedic learning is an altar in the educational system. *Atharva Veda,* is the fourth *Veda,* the storehouse of magical formula, were too a subject in the education, preaching unharmed black magic for the betterment of people and society in the form of hypnosis, telepathy, psycho-kinesis. All the three are proven as a scientific relative theory. The imaginary idea to recreate or invent a new one could be the idea of Transhumanism, a motivational factor. The aircraft is a blueprint of a bird and robot, the human form. The super human is no more a superficial idea of this century. The subjects, imagination and enactment are real myths provoking an adventure or invention. *Frankenstein* or the modern Prometheus by Mary Shelley and *The Invisible Man* by H.G. Wells, *Some Words with Mummy* by Somerset Maugham are few fictional examples of Transhumanist literature.

Mythical and political ideology behind overpowering and conquering states is in the disguise of the movement, Post-colonialism. Evidence from the Aryan Civilisation proves the execution of an unethical ritual *Ashvamedha yajna* or the horse-grazing will. Conquering or claiming a territory and influencing power over people behind the will of an animal and killing at their expense proves the illogical efficiency of a merciless traitor marching the battlefield with a warrior-like being, confronting the battleground for a land.

Adopting a similar ideology, the intruders settled and confiscated the nations slaughtering them. Adding in some references from literature besides the explanation would value the idea of Colonialism in the language of colonisers, resisting the dominance and hegemony to express the oppression. Cultural dominance, hybridity and suppression have rolled their tongues in, making them voiceless. Quoting the expressive lines from "Cattle Thief" by E. Pauline Johnson, would be in place here: "But the threat was scarcely uttered, ere a dozen balls of lead"(1). The line describes the lion-like fearless Cree, the tribal head standing opposite the coloniser when the gunshots pierced him.

Identifying the best polity or defining the administration, the Buddhist are the forefathers formulating it. The political ideology of a state being Republic is well-explained in the Buddhist text in 6 BC. Even though the discovery has major withdrawals implementing the idea to set an ideal empire, the successors have redefined making it successful.

On identifying some pros and cons on this ideology, it is clear and obvious that the rule benefited with responsible, honest and experienced citizens, friendly neighboring states supporting at the time of warfare maintaining culture, art and civilisation. The rule fared well in the exception of power of a traitor. Republicans' defective administration resulted in financial issues, indecisiveness, insecurity, inequality, interference of political parties in state affairs. Attention deficit and delayed response were also a generic ancient issue.

Monarch rule was quite alluring and pathetic with material interest in invading and expanding the empire, and spending the generated revenues of the nation that was earned from agriculture and farming were being invested in the military power. Polygamy was prevalent in the intent of expanding the territory on considering women as mere material possessions and a source for entering into other state affairs. Subjects followed the traitor and devastated the culture.

Foregoing, the setbacks of the 21st century draws attention to the technologies encountering cybercrimes alongside techno improvements. The internet revolution in this millennium had stirred the world with adventures with few insecurities leading to a new idea, Techno Populism, a movement making communication easier. Techno Populism becomes effective with the advent of the internet and social media connecting ordinary men that network with common groups. Populism, a people representative from the political sphere, a leader with his unmasked communication confronted the elites hiding under the political arch. A populist internet savvy, called Techno Populist mediating between the traitor and the enemy is an ancient spy in the past. In short, Techno Populism is a counteractive solution for a two-way communication in the community.

From the ancient text *Manusmriti* considerably a law book and one of the *dharmasastra* texts next to *Vedas* is a reflection of laws and society of the *Mauryan* period from the *Moriyan* tribe, discussing the British Colonial administrators of Kolkata, the early South India. The text has reference to the social class system or varna system. The codes developed by Manu, the political philosopher, the first person of the universe according to Hindu mythology, expresses the Indian political thoughts and has left the first code of civil and criminal laws for the Indians.

Ideologies are a recreation of the doctrines defined in the past. Myth and mythology superficially rule the political world demanding a westernised ambience in a traditional outlook.

Works Cited

Anna, Ceglarska. "The Role of Myth in Political Thought." *Krakowskie Studia z Historii Państwa i Prawa,* vol 11, no.3, 2018, pp.343-355.

Barry, Peter. *Beginning Theory*. Manchester UP, 2009.

Johnson, E. Pauline. "Cattle Thief." http://www.ricenpeas.org.

Tudor, Henry, *Political Myth*, Macmillan P, 1972.

Chapter 12

Ahalya's Awakening: Contemporary Women through Myth

Pooja and Anuradha

I

Myths are a significant part of the culture of any nation and through it one can have a peep into the beliefs and value system of that nation. Mythology is an amalgamation of two Greek words 'mythos' and 'logos', the former means 'speech' or 'discourse' whereas the later means 'fable' or ' legend'. Thus mythology means 'speech of legends'. Literature of our nation *i.e.* India is full of mythological narratives which tell the stories of love, bravery, vengeance, of male as well as female protagonists. In the words of M. Ramya Sri and V.Manimozhi, "Hindu texts present diverse and conflicting views on the position of women, ranging from feminine leadership as the highest goddess to limiting her role to an obedient daughter, housewife and mother"(2). Hence, it is evident that mythological tales are genesis of religion and culture as well.

Ahalya's Awakening (2019) is one of the remarkable novels by eminent novelist Kavita Kane. This exceptional tale is a noteworthy episode present in ancient mythology. Ahalya is the portrayal of a contemporary woman who was silenced by the circumstances and Kavita Kane has given her voice to represent archetypal aspects through varied layers. The story narrates the events much before the curse of Maharishi Gautama, Ahalya's husband gave her due to infidelity. The present study aims at creating responsiveness among women of contemporary era through the voice of the protagonist of the novel. It attempts to re-evaluate the re-presentation of Ahalya in present context. The study also aims at archetypal retelling of social, religious and philosophical aspects in contemporary society.

Furthermore, it discusses the dilemma encountered by Ahalya in her life-long journey towards the development of her inner-self.

Kavita Kane's narratives have made her a social radical who depicts mythological figures as strong as well as thoughtful. She gives her voice to marginalised, misapprehended as well as altered female characters of Indian mythology. Alice Walker has also stated in *Search of Our Mothers' Gardens*, "The writer – like the musician or painter – must be free to explore, otherwise she or he will never discover what is needed (by everyone) to be known. . . . Yet the gift of loneliness is sometimes a radical vision of society or one's people that has not previously been taken into account" (3). She tries to interpret identity and uniqueness of mythological women characters and, through their voice, she attempts to position them in the contemporary society. Her bestselling novel *The Karna's Wife: The Outcast's Queen* (2013) is a reflection of contemporary women as well as artefact of intellectual self-confrontation. Her other works include *Sita's Sister* (2014), *Menaka's Choice* (2015), *Lanka's Princess* (2016), and *The Fisher Queen's Dynasty* (2017). Her works are real depiction of humanist disapproval against magnificent avarice at large and in particular against the patriarchal culture. According to M. Ramya Sri and V.Manimozhi, "Indian feminist begun to step out from the shadow and rewrote mythology, which was written by Man. This was necessary because male discourse elides women. Men written myths have the functions to infantilise women, to irradiate the dysfunction women have to write for themselves in discourse" (5).

Archetypal retellings illuminate and shed new light on the already existing texts in framework of binary situation of present as well as past. *Ahalya's Awakening* is also one such text where Kavita Kane has depicted stone-like existence of a *rishika* as the strongest archetypal figure. Ahalya is a learned *rishika* who has all the knowledge of scriptures and *Vedas*. Kavita Kane has represented her as a woman with flaws and courage to accept whatever comes in her way with grace and elegance. She is a synthesis of traditional mythology and modernity of the current world. She is embedded with moral ethics and values. She knows her culture well and through her knowledge and valour makes place for herself. She is embodiment of conventional principles and her perseverance, passion and liberal mind make her great. Kavita Kane has empowered her with spiritual awakening and comprehension of human aspirations.

Ahalya is the twin sister of Divodasa and is a beautiful daughter of King Mudgala and Nalayani of Puru dynasty. She is the most beautiful woman character of *Ramayana*. Goldman states that the *Bala Kanda* of the *Ramayana* also mentions that Brahma moulds her "with great effort out of pure creative energy" (54).King Mudgal also says at Ahalya's birth, "She is the most beautiful girl on the earth." (*Ahalya's Awakening* 13) Further he tells his wife that on "Lord Brahma's suggestion, Rishi Vashisht decided to name her Ahalya – the beautiful one without blemishes,… But for us, cattle herders who became kings, Ahalya means something deeper, something related to the earth, the soil. Ahalya means the plough, too, when broken into two parts – a-halya, as related to ploughing." (*Ahalya's Awakening* 14) He always sees her daughter as a warrior who is strongest in the dynasty. However, Ahalya's mother Nalayani has other plans for her daughter, she wants to fulfill her own ambitions. She wants that Ahalya should get married to the king of gods and she tells her husband "we have a daughter now. And such a precious, beautiful daughter…She is meant for someone special – someone like Indra, the king of gods" (*Ahalya's Awakening* 16). Here, in the words of Nalayani we can see the significance of women in Indian community. Rishi Vashisht also worries that her parents are more "fascinated by her beauty than her intelligence" (*Ahalya's Awakening* 16).

In the mythological story of *Ramayana* we come to know about Ahalya when Maharishi Vishwamitra, Rama and Lakshmana enter *siddhasharma* and Rama feels holiness of the place. Vishwamitra narrates the story of Maharishi Gautama and Ahalya who had led a life of penance and peace in the *ashram* many years ago. However, Indra spoils the same by committing a sin in the guise of Gautama and eventually Ahalya was cursed to become stone-like figure that will be eradicated by the pious touch of Lord Rama. However, Kavita Kane's narrative begins with a caution when Menaka warns new Indra-Nahusha not to think about marrying Sachi as the cause of previous Indra's downfall was the same. "I have to warn you that you are making the same mistake the previous Indra made" (Prologue *Ahalya's Awakening*). The reason for downfall of king Indra was to keep an eye on Ahalya in R*amayana.* He tried to seduce Ahalya while her husband had gone for a bath.

In the novel, Ahalya is a *rishika* of modern times with a voice of her own as well as an archetypal figure of ancient times. She has been described as a woman who raises her voice with patience and reason as well. She asks many questions to her guru: 'Why is the earth called a mother and not a father?'(*Ahalya's Awakening* 16). She is happy that she has a voice and, in fact, after the question, "she eagerly, heaving a silent sigh of relief that she had been given yet another chance to voice her question" (*Ahalya's Awakening* 16).

Kavita Kane has given voice to *Rishika* and re-presents her as a firm woman and when her mother Nalayani refuses for her education at *Ashram* of Rishi Vashisht, she raises her voice and says, 'Education is never finished, Ma…' (*Ahalya's Awakening* 29). Kavita Kane describes, '…her voice firmer, her composure seemingly unruffled' (*Ahalya's Awakening* 29). Her twin brother also supports her decision and says, "Ma, let her study, … 'She's a brilliant student. And if I have excelled as a warrior, why can she not study what she wants (*Ahalya's Awakening* 30)?" She takes education along with her brother King Divodasa and thus becomes a cerebral *rishika* who has all the knowledge of *Vedas.*

In the due course of the events, Kavita Kane introduces Indra who wants to marry Ahalya, the most beautiful princess on the earth. However, here also Ahalya raises her voice and rejects the proposal to pursue higher studies. She asks Indra, "Does marriage always validate a woman? Or her future?....And then the child's mother, and so on and so forth. Is that all there is to a woman?" (*Ahalya's Awakening* 37) A conversation between Indra and Ahalya in *Ahalya's Awakening* states all the truth about the representation of social status of a woman. When Indra asks, "But … does it not please you at all that you are viewed as the most beautiful woman in the world?... Does that not make you happy?'" (*Ahalya's Awakening* 38). Ahalya asks Indra:

> Should it?...Besides beauty of the body, there is in women beauty of the heart and beauty of the brain, too,' she said. 'But how many see that? Kindness is ignored and intelligence is dismissed. Most would not recognise or acknowledge the wisdom behind loveliness, the wit behind the appealing beauty of a woman. (*Ahalya's Awakening* 38)

She further states would you like it if we viewed men only for their, say, physical strength?' (*Ahalya's Awakening* 38). Similarly, "Women are, likewise, more than just lovely creatures" (*Ahalya's Awakening* 38). Thus she is true archetypal figure who has a choice of her own and is capable enough to make her own decision. She is re-evaluated and re-presented by Kavita Kane as a figure who has reason as well as motivation to pursue her dreams.

Ahalya falls in love with Maharishi Gautama due to his logical abilities and encouraging attitude towards her beliefs. She doesn't feel good about her *swyamvar* which was planned by her family. Although eventually Maharishi Gautma wins the race and her mother tells her 'I came here to let you know that Rishi Gautam has won your hand by circumambulating a cow' (*Ahalya's Awakening* 119). She redeems with joy and says 'That I love him and he loves me; that's why he came here!' (*Ahalya's Awakening* 120).

She had a happy married life with Rishi Gautama and was blessed with four kids. She used to live a happy life as wife of a guru and used to teach other pupils in *ashram* too. On the other hand, Rishi Gautama was busy in his daily chores of educating scriptures and *Vedas* to the new entrants. Their life became monotonous and King Indra took benefit of the same. In the words of Renate Sohnen Thieme, "Such a beautiful woman is naturally desired by the other gods too; Brahma, however, decides to entrust her to the celebrated sage Gautama for education, and finally to marry her to him, at which point India in particular, becomes enraged. …Indra's motive for intruding into Ahalya's married life is obviously jealousy or envy of Gautama" (50).

King Indra came to seduce the *rishika* and Ahalya too fell to it for a moment meanwhile Mahrishi Gautama enters the room and curses Indra at the moment but refuses to curse *rishika* as he himself blames for their monotonous life. He asks Ahalya, 'You broke that love, that trust, Ahalya. Will my forgiveness ever restore it all?' (*Ahalya's Awakening* 238) She answers 'We all do what we think is expected of us,…You were always the guru, and I was the wife of a guru, never *your* wife, Gautam. I don't think I was ever yours' (*Ahalya's Awakening* 239).

Maharishi gautam reminds her about her dream of becoming a *rishika* and tells her that she hasn't become one still as her emotions have controlled her mind and body as well. "You have lost in becoming a devoted mother and a wife while you have forgotten to search for peace and illumination you had always hoped for" (*Ahalya's Awakening* 244).He then states his last words, "May you remain invisible to the human eye but visible in your mind's eye, surviving on air and lying in ashes till the time you receive your blessing, your enlightenment, Ahalya" (*Ahalya's Awakening* 244). He said softly. "In that quest you shall receive your salvation – the deliverance you searched for so long all these years" (*Ahalya's Awakening* 244).

She becomes a stone and meanwhile searches for her true self. In later years, Lord Rama enters her *ashram* and eradicates her curse. Meanwhile Rishi Gautama too enters in the *ashram* after years and feels apology for his deeds. However, as she has now become a true *rishika* after years of penance, she refuses to leave with Rishi Gautama and remains there itself. The novel ends with an epilogue where Sita and Ahalya meet each other and discuss their lives and curses. Ahalya says, "I have turned my curse into a blessing by becoming *rishika* in true sense" (*Ahalya's Awakening* 255). She says, "I searched all these years for myself – and I only found Ahalya, the woman I was supposed to be born as: unblemished, without any faults. I had no hala in me, no sin, no crime, no guilt. What I had done was to respond to the call of life within me ..." (*Ahalya's Awakening* 255). Sita also depicts that she doesn't take herself as a victim as well and it is for her own honour and pride that she left the kingdom. No one has asked her to leave it and it was her decision to leave the palace for sake of the kingdom itself. Hence, their actions communicate that it is not important for women's identity to cater completely to the men's desires.

Thus, to conclude, we can state that in *Ahalya's Awakening,* Ahalya is not a victim. She is a courageous woman who is not scared to accept her flaws; she is aware of her desires, transgression and the consequences. She has chosen a path of self – reliance and glor. She is a warrior who fought back like a true *rishika.* Nowhere in the whole story Kavita Kane has represented her as a sufferer rather she has been portrayed as a protagonist who has attained her zeal for education and power. She herself requests to her guru 'I want to try the bow and arrows today' (*Ahalya's Awakening* 18). Ahalya is an epitome of optimism and confidence as she is self-reliant who always achieves what she believes. She may have faced diverse situations but she has always arises like a phoenix. Aishwarya Sahasrabudhe also states: "*Ahalya's Awakening*... traces the paradox of its eponymous protagonist, who is "deemed promiscuous", and yet, is seen as a symbol of chastity" (1). She symbolises hope for all the women in contemporary era and suggests that to become self-reliant is more significant for one's growth and development. The last words of Kavita Kane are noteworthy, "Ahalya smiled. His words came clearly to her as she sat with Sita on the veranda, feeling the hot sun on her face, soaking in the sense of self-fulfilment she had never had before. She was ... Ahalya" (*Ahalya's Awakening* ...)

Works Cited

Goldman, Robert P. *The Ramayana of Valmiki: Balakanda. The Ramayana of Valmiki: An Epic of Ancient India.* Vol. 1. Princeton UP. 1990.

Kane, Kavita. *Ahalya's Awakening.* Westland, 2019.

Ramya Sri M. and V. Manimozhi. "A Study of Perspective Writing with Reference to Kavita Kane's *Sita's Sister. Malaya Journal of Matematik*, vol. 1, no. 2, 2020, pp. 4896-4901.

Sahasrabudhe, Aishwarya. "In *Ahalyas Awakening*, Kavita Kané Questions the Penalty for Infidelity, and Its Significance in Indian Mythology." https://doi.org/10.26637/MJM0S20/1265.

Walker, Alice. *In Search of Our Mothers' Gardens: Womanist Prose.* Phoenix, 2005.

Thieme, Renate Sohnen. "The Ahalya Story through the Ages." *Myth and Myth Making Continous Evolution in Indian Tradition*, edited by Julia Leslie, Routledge, 1996, pp. 39-65.

Chapter 13

Retelling the Myth of American Dream in Arthur Miller's *Death of a Salesman*

Pooja Goyal

Arthur Miller(1915-2005) has invariably been acclaimed as one of the few American writers who looked at American Dream as something that influenced not only the political and economic policies of America but also the mindset of common citizens to look ahead and extend constructive contribution in the progress of the United States of America. This paper explores and critically evaluates Miller's critique of American Dream in *Death of a Salesman.* An allied area of enquiry will be to examine how it adversely affects the lives of common people who believed in the celebrated ideals of equality, fraternity and justice in a democratic America. It, however, would be pertinent to look at the concept of American Dream and its various dimensions as well as its conceptual and historical interpretation before analysing it in the play in question.

A person can change himself into a personality if he sets certain high goals of his life and achieves them; nevertheless, in case his goals or dreams are illusionary or fake and unable to achieve, his whole life can be reduced to 'aridiculouslie.' Such is the life of common Americans who are shown a dream of millions but they do not get even pennies. The earlier settlers in America fled the tensions of their old worlds to seek a better life in the New World with boundless opportunities. They considered America as a 'Holy Land' as God created it for them. "America became 'the place,' Carpenter opines, where there ligious prophecies of Isaiah and The Republican ideals of Plato might be realised" (6). Slowly and steadily such aspirations for attaining an economically successful and religiously puritanical life to ok a shape of legendary status and gave birth to the myth of American Dream. Guerin argues in this connection:

> The central facet of this myth cluster is the Myth of Edenic Possibilities, which reflects the hope of creating a second paradise, not in the next world and not outside time, but in the bright New World of the American Continent. . . . a place where human beings, after centuries of poverty, misery and corruption, could have a second chance to fulfil their mythic yearnings for are turn to paradise(186).

However, later on, for the poor white men, black people, women and minorities, America proved to be a demonic land where they came to struggle incessantly and also found their dreams of prosperity shattered.

If the concept of American Dream as a termanda movement is taken together, one finds that it has been completely idealised as well as exploited from one President of US to the other like Thomas Jefferson to Joe Biden. All United States Presidents have continued to revive America as a dreamy land, but many economists and literary writers have declared it a continuous decline. The postmodernist American novelists like Saul Bellow, Norman Mailer, Joseph Heller, John Updike, Philip Roth and many others doubt the notion of prosperity in America as unequal distribution of wealth, domestic-racial discrimination and corrupt greedy political and capitalist systems are the biggest threats to American creed of unity, integrity and thus, progress.

The concept of American Dream has also its roots in the national ideals set up by Thomas Jefferson, the first President of America:

> By the late eighteenth century, America's self-image, its political creed, was set. Thomas Jefferson, Benjamin Franklin, John Adams, and their revolutionary colleagues in the Congress of 1776 grounded the new nation's in dependence on the declaration "that all Men are created equal, that they are endowed by their Creator with certain unalienable Rights that among these are Life, Liberty, and the Pursuit of Happiness (Jillson 3).

But these ideals prove to be mythical and thus doubtful in their nature and function. Since her independence on July 4, 1776, America had remained a land of feuds and wars among her people: a civil war happened between the white and the black communities during the years of 1861 to 1865. Anti-slavery, suffrage, feministic and various human rights movements have always prevalent in the US. The basic reason behind it is that the others might have a supreme place in the society, but a commoner has always a limited and subordinate place. It means that the political leaders of the country are not so honest and true in their working aspect that the commoners have to come on roads to actualise their rights and enjoy the same privilege of the streamlined rich whitemen.

The meaning of American Dream has changed with the changing historical and literary periods in America. During the time of American Renaissance or early National period from1776 to 1830, the writers like Washington Irving, James Fennimore Cooper and Charles Brockden Brown linked it with the unity and integrity of people:

> The grand promise of the American Dream has always been that those willing to learn, work, save, persevere, and play by the rules will have a better chance to grow and prosper in America than anywhere else on earth. Still, as Walter Lippmann said more than a century ago (and as quoted in the epigraph to this preface), the dream needs regularly to be re-examined, criticized, and even challenged, to ensure that it still marks the way to a future that serves the real needs and interests of our nation and its people (Jillson ix).

Following these ideals, in American Romantic age from 1830-1870 there came the writers who brought forth the vision of liberty basically for the blacks, women and children. Ralph Waldo Emerson, Henry David Thoreau, Nathaniel Hawthorne and Walt Whitman projected this idea through their literary works. In the age of Realism from 1871 to 1910, the novelists like William Dean Howells and Mark Twain questioned the concepts of slavery and freedom in America. A new dream emerged here in the form of taking education and getting succeeded. In the modern age (1910-1940), new developments of science brought industrialisation which brought a new dream of economic independence, but that also brought a new kind of exploitation of labour class depicted in many plays of Eugene O' Neill, Arthur Miller and Tennessee Williams as also in the novels of F. Scott Fitzgerald, John Steinback, Ernest Hemingway, William Falkner and many more. But throughout from the establishment of the new world in America till today, American Dream remains an illusionary concept beyond reach and reality. Cal Jillson says, "Race, gender, wealth, ethnicity, and religion have all been used to exclude persons and groups from the community of American citizens" (7). He adds:

> Our most prominent novelists–Nathaniel Hawthorne, Herman Melville, Mark Twain, Theodore Dreiser, Sinclair Lewis, William Faulkner, John Steinbeck, John Updike, Toni Morrison, and Philip Roth, among many others–have warned of the dangerous implausibility of the American

> Dream. The great characters of our national fiction, including Hester Prynne, Captain Ahab, Huckleberry Finn, George Babbitt, Bigger Thomas, Seymour "the Swede" Levov, and Miles Roby, remind us that victories and defeats, dreams and nightmares, all are common to the human experience. Politicians declare that America offers opportunity to all who will prepare well, work hard, save, and invest, but novelists warn, in Kurt Vonnegut's memorable phrase, that most people are "the listless playthings of enormous forces" (Jillsonx).

Though America has outwardly attained the position of a super-power among other nations, however, inwardly it is still pursuing Thomas Jefferson's idea of "equality, liberty and pursuit of happiness" for all its citizens and tries to become "a shining city on the hill" (Bush 145) and also a light for others.

Challenging the myth of America as an ideal land for a common man, Arthur Miller's Death of a Salesman (1949) finds Americans reaching their intellectual, spiritual and economicnadiron one hand and in a ditch of many tragic incidents both personal and social on the other. This play is hailed as 'a modern tragedy' revealing the plight of the poor commoners and proletarians in the hands of rich bourgeois in America. Arthur Miller himself says "I believe that the common man is as apt as a subject for tragedy in its highest sense as king were" (*Tragedy* 1). In the play, Willy Loman (as his surname suggests 'low man') is presented as the tragic anti-hero representing economically the lower strata of society with his ambitious nature, massive dreams and turbulent longings to establish his own business in future. He says to both of his sons, Biff and Happy, "You, Hapand I, and I'll show you all the towns. America is full of beautiful town sand fine, upstanding people" (*Death of a Salesman* 2122); nevertheless he becomes a prey in the hands of the rich people of same towns of America. Moreover, His house has an "air of the dream clings to the place, a dream rising out of reality" (*Death of a Salesman* 2111). However, this reality seems 'unreal' as this dream of boundless opportunities never gets realised for the Loman family. Willy is presented as "a man halflostin the American dream, a man who is unable to tell past from present. Perhaps the play should have been called *The Dying of a Salesman,* because Willy is dying throughout" (Bloom 5). The chief quality of Arthur Miller is his courage to challenge the untruth, his humanism and a deep compassion for the weak and the oppressed. In Greek tragedy, man is a victim of mysterious forces of the fate beyond his control, but in modern tragedy, in realistic sense of the term, undoubtedly the forces of capitalist and commercial values are shown in their true colors converting an innocent person in to a dupe like Willy Loman in the play.

Autobiographically, the play is based on Miller's own experiences of the period of 'Great Depression' (1929-39) in America. Arthur Miller was born in 1915, in New York. His father, who had emigrated from Austria at the age of six, was a successful coat manufacturer and his mother was a school teacher. They were the rich persons living in large apartment. Miller's family was an embodiment of the American Dream that hard work is always rewarded. The character of Willy Loman in the play Death of a Salesman seems based on Miller's own father who supported American ideals in his earlier life. But the stock market crash of 1929 changed everything and the sad period of economic depression came on the surface that uncovered them ask of American Dream. The business started getting lost. There was poverty, unemployment and corruption all around. The Miller family was forced to shift to the poor Flat bush section of Brooklyn in a small frame house. His father never fully recovered from his business failure and his mother was often depressed and embittered by the family's poverty. Both were in hope of an economic recovery. From those critical days, Miller started telling the hollowness and fragility of the American Dream of economic success and the social justice; He also achieved many rewards from this play particularly Pulitzer Prize for Dramain 1949. Biff in the play *Death of a Salesman* appears the alter-ego of Arthur Miller himself who rejects all the flimsy American dreams altogether.

The previous title of the play "Inside One's Head" and the subtitle" Certain Private Conversations in Two Acts and a Requiem" indicate that the tragic action of the play is a clash between the individual and the modern society. It is devoted to the depressed internal mind of Willy and the projection of his memories of idyllic past through his confessional speeches, stream of consciousness, hallucinations and flash back techniques. Willy is unable to bear with the modern commodification of culture. The cutting of elm trees round his home makes him 'unhappy', for along with his sons he used to enjoy the trees in his past. The 'peripeteia' of his life has already taken place before the play begins as Willy is shown living a posthumous existence in his sixties and the victim of schizophrenia accompanied by the failure and also disillusionment in his professional life as a salesman and private life as a husband and a father. Sometimes, he used to talk to himself and sometimes to his sons, friends and relatives altogether in his imagination. Willy says "I' mtired to the death. I couldn't make it" (*Death of a Salesman* 2112). In such an old age, for selling of his company's products, he has to drive his own car from New York to Yonkers in New England with an average of sixtymiles an hour. His words on American life display his utter frustration: There's more people! That's ruining the country! Population is getting out of control. The competition is maddening (*Death of a Salesman* 2115).

Willy believes in the success-oriented society but finds financial success a mirage there. The less capable he is becoming as a businessman, the more success attracts him. Throughout the play, Willy along with his sons try to adjust in a confused American business culture which only shows the vision of successful men, but does not show the ways how to get success.

Moreover, Biff and Happy grow up as the two average non-entities who eradicate their father's desires to see them the personalities of greatness and grandeur. Willy's expression for Biff "Not finding yourself at the age of thirty-four is a disgrace!" (*Death of a Salesman* 2114) totally collapses the dreams of a father who thinks high of his children with "personal attractiveness" and doing "simonizing job" for him in their adolescent age (*Death of a Salesman* 2114). Bifffeels contented in his farm job, but cannot happily continue it because of his father's modest and sophisticated business ethics. He tells Happy, "There's nothing more inspiring or – beautiful than the sight of a mare and a new colt" (*Death of a Salesman* 2117). But at the same time he feels dissatisfied for not getting a sophisticated job in a company according to the expectations of Willy who often says, "Personality always wins the day" (*Death of a Salesman* 2139). Biff says:

> I've had twenty or thirty different kinds of jobs since I left home before thewar, and it always turns out the same. I just realised it lately. In Nebraska when I herded the cattle, and the Dakotas, and Arizona, and now in Texas. It's why I came home now, I guess, because I realised it. . . . I'm not getting anywhere! What the hell am I doing, playing around with horses, twenty-eight dollarsa week! I'm thirty-four years old. I oughta be makin' my future (*Death of a Salesman* 2117).

Happy also says about his dilemma, "See, Biff, everybody around me is so false that I'm constantly lowering my ideals..." (*Death of a Salesman* 2118). In the play, the clash between them represents a clash between the two sets of cultural values – the old and the agrarian; the new and the industrial. One who is rooted in the agrarian values can neither understand nor reject the other who is steeped into the competitive values of a modern industrialised age.

Willy, on the other hand, repeatedly thanks Almighty for his sons particularly Biff built "Like a young god. Hercules" (*Death of a Salesman* 2141) in America, a land of power and prosperity. He teaches them, "Start big, you'll end big" (*Death of a Salesman* 2139), but his extravagant speeches derogatively affect the psyche and career of his children. Biff says, "And I never got anywhere because you blew me so full of hot air I could never stand taking orders from anybody! That's whose faultitis!"(*Death of a Salesman* 2172). Biff who remains Willy's ultimate hope of success, his failure shakes up Willy so badly that he mumbles and laughs like a crazy man in the dark and depressed realm. He tells Biff that the world is an oyster, but he does not crack it open on a mattress. For Willy, Biff is just wasting his life on the farm and Happy is not happy with his worldly achievements of "an apartment, a car and plenty of women" (*Death of a Salesman* 2118) in a money-worshiping society as Happy us ually says, "And still goddammit, I' mlonely" (*Death of a Salesman* 2118).

The play not only projects the miserable life of a poor white American man but alsoquestions the wretched conditions of the US women who are considered as muted creatures having no rights of their own. Linda Loman, the wife of Willy, represents a suppressed domestic womanhood, easily cuckolded, unable to venther feelings and often seen serving the family. When the play opens, Miller describes the personality of Linda:

> Most often jovial, she has developed an iron repression of her exceptions to Willy's behavior–she more than loves him, admires him, as though hismercurial nature, his temper, his massive dreams and little cruelties, servedher only as sharp reminders of the turbulent longings within him, longingwhich she shares but lacks the temperament to utter and follow to their end (*Death of a Salesman* 2112).

Moreover, like another domestic traditional woman, Linda is an idealised portrait of a wife who adores her husband and often rebukes her sons for not caring their father:

> Willy Loman never made a lot of money. His name was never in the paper. He's not the finest character that ever lived. But he's a human being, and a terrible thing is happening to him. So attention must be paid. He's not allowed to fall into his grave like an old dog . . . (*Death of a Salesman* 2134).

Linda, who remains a great support to Willy, never gets what she deserves as his wife. Whats he gets is the other woman in the life of Willy.

Throughout his life, though Willy tries to project an inflated image of himself in a bid to impress his sons and the outer world, he fails in doing so. Moreover, his one mistake of making love to another woman also brings down his false edifice. The character of this woman in the play works manifold, It enhances its tragic effect by putting Willy into one more difficult and desperate situation before Biff and shows Willy's relation with his sexless motherly wife and also highlights the patriarchal attitude of American men considering a woman 'a body' or 'acommodity'. Lois Tyson asserts in this connection:

> The Lomans' sexual attitudes intersect in what is known in common parlance as the "good girl/bad girl" view of women. "Good girls" are virgins until marriage; therefore, they are the girls men marry. "Bad girls" do not confine their sexual activity to marriage; therefore, they are the girls men sleep with, hold in contempt, and sooner or later abandon. Obviously, the salesman and his sons enact this attitude in their talk about and behavior toward women....This is the pre-1960s sexual attitude associated with the social and political conservatism of post-World War II America, and clearly, it served the patriarchal status quo by maintaining maledomination over women physically and psychologically....their social role provides them with the psychological escape they seek. Willy doesn't have to ask himself why he cheated on his wife; Happy doesn't have to probe too deeply in to his motives for stealing othermen's fiancées; Biff doesn't have to wonder why he used to be so rough with the girls who threw themselves at him in highs chool (78-79).

Arthur Miller, however, shows the consequences of such sexual encounters like Willy in his guilt consciousness continuously listens to the laughter of this woman (in darkness) that makes him disturbed all the time. The presence of this woman "in her sliponly" in the hotel room of Willy in the city of Boston, Willy's giving her the stockings which Linda desperately needs and his acceptance of sexual indulgence with the woman cause a big shock to Biff (who suddenly comes in the room in his desperation) that shuns the idealised image of his father. Bernard, Biff's friend, tells Willy about the mentally disturbed condition of Biff after the incident:

> And he came back after that month and took his sneakers – remember thoses neakers with "University of Virginia" printed on them? He was so proud of them, wore them everyday. And he took them down in the cellar, and burned the mup in the furnace (*Death of a Salesman* 2153).

Biff does not re-appear in the subject of Mathematics and oscillates from one job to another and wanders here and there like "a philandering bum" (*Death of a Salesman* 2135) as Linda says about him. He starts staying away from home. Linda remarks, "Biff, a man is not a bird, to come and go with the spring time" (*Death of a Salesman* 2134). Biff begins to steal wherever he goes. His going to jail for such a deed throws cold water on Willy's dream for Biff as a successful business man. He openly starts saying about Willy, "He's got no character" (*Death of a Salesman* 2134). He further says that Willy throws him out of the house "...Because I know he's a fake and he doesn't like anybody around who knows" (*Death of a Salesman* 2135) abou this relationship with another woman.

Willy's reverie of happy homely and professional life represents the Biblical myth of Eden Garden in which Willy Loman is an archetypal fallen Adam. He tries to eke out his living and find happiness but is misunderstood and never succeeds to please the God of success. Biff and Happy remind one of their responsible sons of Adam – Ca in and Abel. In the play, Willy works incessantly and has to stay away from his family for many days sometimes and the companyof another woman as his lover seems a reliever to him from stress and tiredness for somemoments. Willy reasons before Biff, "I was terribly lonely" (*Death of a Salesman* 2117). On the other, Willy is actually at war with his innercompulsions and outer forces which the innocent mind of Biff can not understand. Biff destroys himself for the sake of marital rights of his mother.

The collapse of the family – the so called prism of the society – represents the collapse of the whole society and the myth of American dream. For Willy, home is a place when one goes in, it takes one in. However, home is presented here as a hostile alienated world without any care and love from his children. Willy expresses his despair on this situation, "Work a life time to pay off a house, you finally own it and there is no body to live in it" (*Death of a Salesman* 2114). The modern projection of desperate homes having insensitive attitude of its family members and uncomfortable life directly challenges the ancestral fairy tale like stories of Americans' happy homely lives. Inspite of it, Willy puts his whole life into Biff, pawns his watch fob with a diamond for Biff's radio correspondence course and tries to kill himself twice for his insurance money to his sons (first by smashing his car and secondly by gassing himself), but Biff turns his back on Willy. Willy's life is surrounded by the broken images like broken refrigerator, washing machine, smashing of his car symbolic of his broken relationship with his sons. He says, "I am always in race with junkyard" (*Death of a Salesman* 2142).

Willy fails to adopt any of the three alternative paths to success provided by the three persons in the play. First, his idea of getting rich quickly through personality is personified by his brother Ben, an adventurer having diamond mines. Ben often tells his success-story in the words, ". . . when I was seventeen I walked into the jungle, and when I was twenty-one, I walked out and by God I was rich" (*Death of a Salesman* 2130). Secondly, Willy does not want his sons to be like uncle Charley having small business in comparison to that of Ben. He wishes his sons the supposed legendary fearless characters who should treat the world as a forest and grab whatever they can. But all in vain. His plan does not work out. Thirdly, theinfluence of Dave Singleman, a successful salesman at the age of 84 having "drummed merch and is einthirty-one states" (*Death of a Salesman* 2146) expresses his sense of success in a sales man's business. Contrary to it, Willy seems failed because of his aging factor.

Willy also presents a contrast between present and past of business morality. He says, "There was a respect and comradeship and gratitude in it. Today, it is all cut and dried, and there's no chance for bringing friendship to bear–or personality" (*Death of a Salesman* 2147). Willy, who has now become an old and senile one, is no longer needed in the firm. Moreover, instead of getting old age security, he is forced to work on a straight commission. Wllly's burst sums up a man's helplessness and his exploitation at the hands of the capitalist class. Heoutcries, I put thirty-four years into this firm, Howard and now I can't pay my insurance! You can't eat the orange and throw the peel away – a man is not a piece of fruit (*Death of a Salesman* 2147).

He feels completely shattered. The tragedy becomes bigger when the Loman family manages to whip itself into a false excitement about Happy's ideal scheme of selling sporting goods. Happy in his excitement says:

> We form two basketball teams, see? Two water-polo teams. We play each other. It's a million dollars' worth of publicity. Two brothers, see? The Loman brothers. Displays in the Royal Palms–all the hotel. And banners over the ring and the basketball court: "Loman Brothers." Baby, we could sell porting goods! (*Death of a Salesman* 2138).

In comparison to Biff, Happy seems following the dreamy path of the father. Willy says to Biff and Happy, "You guys together could absolutely lick the civilised world" (*Death of a Salesman* 2138). Thereafter, Willy is shown sleeping like a dead one after a long span of time. But unfortunately, the scheme is never implemented. Willy than escapes into the world of pastoral bliss from the harshness of his life. The desire of planting seeds symbolises his growing fear that he will die without any roots in the ground. Willy's real dichotomy lies in between the fact and the falsehood of his illusions.

Death is left for him a lastres or to repaying price for his family's happiness, for his death can bring his insurance money of twenty thousand dollars to his family. And it is also an escape for himself. He retorts "Does it take more guts to stand here the rest of my life, ringing up a zero? (*Death of a Salesman* 2169). When Biff at the height of his emotional outburst breaksdown into weeping and embraces Willy, a strange satiety comes to Willy. He makes his mind to do something better for Biff. Willy leaves twenty thousand dollars of his insurance money to Biff after his death. He commits suicide by smashing his own car and himself. Willy before his death in his hallucination says, "Ben, he'll [Biff] worship me for it" (*Death of a Salesman* 2174). However, Biff still blames Willy and his "phony" and "wrong dreams" (*Death of a Salesman* 2175). His suicide can be taken as an act of supreme sacrifice for his children and the assertion of his dream of success for his sons along with his identity and dignity before both of them. One can consider that his suicide is actually the last fight to realise his past dream in the present. Eric J. Sterling argues:

> Willy's fight reaches beyond himself and his family, and essentially becomes a larger, more communal struggle to revive the pastoral dream of an America that is fading into the sunset. This fight becomes a battle for the preservation of his version of the American Dream. He fights for recognition, for attention, for respect, for dignity, for love, and for immortality. Willy struggles to rebuild the dream that is no longer available to his children. He longs to passion a tradition that he believes will offer them hope for the future (55).

After his death, his wife makes the last payment on the house where "there'll be nobody home" (*Death of a Salesman* 2176). The "Requiem" over the dead shows the Loman family and Charley paying homage to Willy: Linda is full of remorse and Happy tries to step into the shoes of his father by adopting the same business of sales manship.

In the "Requiem", Charley's remarks about the salesman, Willy Loman, depicts everyman's perennial predicament in the modern society:

> Willy was a salesman. And for a salesman, there is no rock bottom to the life. He don't put a bolt to a nut. He didn't tell you the law or give you medicine. He's a man wayout there in the blue, riding on a smile and as hoeshine. And when they start not smiling back – that's an earth-quake. . . . Nobody dast blame this man. A salesman is got to dream, boy (*Death of a Salesman* 2175).

In the play, the real conflict is between Willy as a man and a salesman in this business world. He, at the end, has to sell his own life to save the life of his family. Willy's death is a direct consequence of his romantic illusionary ideals of Americ and ream belonging mainly to successful economic life which seems deeply instilled in to the psyche of all Americans.

Works Cited

Bloom, Harold, editor. *Arthur Miller*. Chelsea House, 2007.

Bush, Melanie E. L. "What 'American' Dream?: Contemporary Reflections." *The Routledge Handbook on the American Dream,* edited by Robert C. Hauhart and Mitja Sardoc, vol II. Routledge, 2023, pp. 134-152.

Carpenter, Frederic I. *American Literature and the Dream.* Philosophical Library, 1959.

Guerin, Wilfred L, et al., editors. *A Handful of Critical Approaches.* Oxford UP, 1992.

Jillson, Cal. *The American Dream in History, Politics and Fiction.* University P, 2016.

Miller, Arthur. *Death of a Salesman. The Norton Anthology of American Literature,* edited by Nina Baym, vol. E, W.W. Norton, 2003.

---. *Tragedy and the Common Man.* https://acikders.ankara.edu.tr›resource›view. Accessed 10 Dec. 2022.

Sterling, Eric J. *Arthur Miller's* Death of a Salesman. Amsterdam, 2008.

Tyson, Lois. *Psychological Politics of the American Dream.* Ohio State UP, 1994.

Chapter 14

Formation of Myths about Colonial Indian Railways: A Nineteenth Century Review

Sudipta Sardar

Railways had always been a fascinating phenomenon since its inception in the beginning of nineteenth century. Railways never failed to amuse the masses around it and those who would be traveling by it. Railways influenced the social living parameters and social, economical structures in a very crucial way. Hence there had been a prolific amount of importance given to the railways. As a consequence of such importance, railways soon found its place in literature, history and folklore traditions. Through such account railways were found to be portrayed in myriad manners. There were mythical represent of trains in literature, sometimes as venomous serpent sweeping through the jungles and most often as a heavenly creature whistling away its coming. Trains played a crucial part in movies and stories also, where trains were not only an iron scrap object but a living being. During the colonial period in India, trains were the top most scientific innovation which the Britishers introduced in India. And since the inauguration of the railways, it became a fascinating object for the Indian masses also.

Several educationally deprived people used to gaze at the coming trains with fearful glee and considered it as the coming of joy and happiness. Very soon the railways found it in the folklores, often represented as a creature of another world, as if the train was a Leviathan. The railways in colonial India was perhaps nothing but a myth in fulfilling the long thriving desire of democracy. The railways, a considered gift from Britain, also became a myth when it turned out to be tool of capitalism. The railways within its very structure consisted or perhaps created a myth for unity amidst diversity and very deliberately looked promising for connecting India in an explicit manner. Also in Gandhian viewpoint trains were mythically found to be a social construct. However, by the end of colonialism the trains took the shape of a blood train and became a horrific object of religious and cultural animosity.

This paper intends to bring forward how the colonial railways transformed into myth and what were the myths circulating about the colonial railways under the British government in India. This paper would also highlight how the railways became a thing of wonder or Leviathan by the Indian society. An attempt is also made to bring out the caste myth about the railways. This paper would also discuss about the myriad ways railways was projected in the Indian literature during the colonial period. This paper would also point out how the considered gift of railways to India from Britain turned out to be a myth and how railways turned out to be capitalist tool or was it a capitalist tool only. There had been a very particular myth regarding this phenomenon among the colonial apologists about that. This paper would also show how the railways, considered by Gandhi as a social construct, became a blood train and became the witness of such horrific accounts of partition.

To begin the discussion about the formation of myth about the railways during the colonial period we need to remember how the railways were seen in the European and American societies where it was first established. The railways in Europe brought about a significant amount of social changes and in the lives of people around it. The railways not only brought happiness but also quickened the pace of development. Because of the railways there was a rapid transport of goods and materials from one corner to another for a very cheap price than earlier. In America, the rhythmical running sounds of the railway tracks amused and soothed people around it. The railways at one point became the sole carrier of happiness and prosperous future amidst jungles of America. Henry David Thoreau in his poetry book *Walden,* talked about the railways which were the sole promise of the coming of a civilisation in America. Likewise Walt Whitman also sang praises about the railways and in his poems railways often took the mythical shape of a destroyer, cutting through the inhabitable jungles of America and making them habitable in a very swift and peaceful manner. The trains in Europe and America were thus a mythical representation of the wish for a prosperous civilisation wrought with equality. But very soon the heavenly creature, which the railways was portrayed, turned out to be a capitalist tool and during the war those trains became a haunting grunt of a devil which sought to destroy civilisation.

Likewise, in India, the introduction of the railways fascinated the Indian masses that looked at it like a tiny spectator gazing upon the coming and departure of the railways like a Leviathan. The railways among the educationally deprived masses and illiterate people of India was a thing of wonder, at point even they became very superstitious. To them the railways was a fascinating object and a great prospect for amusement. In the movies also the same kind of zeal and amusement about the coming of railways could be seen. In the movies such as *Apu Trilogy*, the railways was the carrier of great joy and satisfaction, the projection of railways in this movie not only celebrated togetherness but also a positive vibe of pleasure.

At the time of the introduction of railways in the 1850's colonial India, most of the upper caste members were prejudiced about the railways working prowess. They were suspicious about the railway traveling because the railway incorporated within it a number of carriages which had several classes and compartments according to that. And the upper caste Indians thought that traveling with the lower caste and outcaste members in the same train attached with several bogies carrying them as well would pollute them and harm their sanctity. Thus the upper caste members always hesitated to travel by the train in those days. This kind of approach and outlook of the upper caste members was very mythical in nature which had no such basis of impurities in it to travel with such men in the train. However, it was true that during the initial phases, the railway companies failed to attract upper caste members to travel by train. Hence, passenger trains found more numbers of middle class and lower class members rather than the upper caste members. Even if some of the upper caste members tried to travel in the first class or second class compartments, they were brutally humiliated by the Britishers and other foreigners for their ethnicity and mannerism. Hence, there was a dark side as well. Nonetheless, it was a myth that travelling with the outcaste members in the same train would pollute them. None of the religious scriptures such as *Manu Smriti* or any other text never really backed up this concept of the upper caste members and hence such perception was always faulty and harmful for the society's stability as well.

It needed to be mentioned that a few of the upper caste members thought it otherwise and apprehended that the railway could play a crucial role in uniting India and could have brought in social equality and justice. They believed that the attached bogies of the railway carrying men from different strata of the society not only brought them closer but also gave a fellow compassion. And even travelling with the foreigners in the same train could have sent the Indian society a message of equality and balance in the society. But a deeper look inside the reality and aftermath of such railway management would brought to light that the trains were introduced in India not with the purpose of connecting Indian people but to connect each corner of the country and making transport easier and quicker, but the trains were not intended to create a cross-cultural bond. It was rather established to gain profit by it and send goods and raw material to Britain for their own usage and consumption. Hence, it was only a myth that the railways would bring forward a state of equality and cross-cultural bond. A deeper look inside the recorded experiences of the travelers and the discrepancy faced by the Indian travelers of all sorts of strata would disclose actual state of the matter.

Post-colonial studies of the railway's management and working systems disclosed many facts about transporting quite a huge amount of goods to England. The railways, in fact, helped them increase their pace of loot in India. However, it needed to be mentioned that the great loot was not totally outside the views of the educated Indians. But they were helpless in such conditions as all forces were against them and the complete authority was on the side of the private companies of the Britishers. Hence, the railways in post-colonial studies had been seen as a serpent of the Britishers eating away and poisoning the Indian resources and its people. But the apologists for empire like to claim that the British brought democracy, the rule of law and trains to India. Governor General Lord Hardinge argued in 1843 that the railways would be beneficial 'to the commerce, government and military control of the country'. But all such things turned out to be a myth that was fed to the innocent Indian masses for the establishment of their capitalist tool. In their very perception and construction, the Indian railways was a colonial scam. For that to happen, the Government paid guaranteed double returns to the investors but it needed to be remembered that all those returns were paid from Indian treasury and not from the Britishers treasury.

Arup K. Chatterjee in his book *The Purveyors of Destiny: A Cultural Biography of the Indian Railways* commented that the railways "is not just an actually existing entity, but is, rather, a myth of tremendously Indian proportions, invoked and evoked in all forms of the national and popular imagination"(64). This statement by Arup K. Chatterjee did provide the actuality of the benefits that India received from the colonial rulers along with democracy and law. But we could never ignore the fact that the initial promise of the railways to provide benefit to the Indian masses did become successful but it was that the Britishers and their private companies fetched much more profit than the Indians. Rather, it was a colonial scam because they knew they had to blind the Indians with a little benefit to gather more benefit from it. Hence it would not be wrong to proclaim that the proposition of the railways were like the business proposal which later on turned them to be the absolute ruler of the nation, likewise the railways also slowly turned out to be a colonial tool of capitalism and a mechanism to loot India.

The railways had long being considered as a marvelous scientific invention that could only bear fruits and develop a country's socio-economic growth. However, as already been mentioned, the railways in colonial India turned out to be a complete myth in terms of the general development of the country. In Gandhian viewpoint, the railways were seen as a social construct. According to Gandhi it was a promising prospect for the future generation. But little did he know that the colonial railways were actually turning out to be a capitalist tool to rob India from its wealth.

However, before criticizing the entirety of the railway system established by the Colonial rulers, we need to keep in mind that the railways did played a crucial part in the development of India, not only in the technological advances but also in the socio-economic and cultural development. Because of the railways, it was possible to connect India and it was easier to form unison through the rapid transportation of the railways under the colonial reign. Hence, amidst such circumstances and even with such great amount of financial depression that the railway caused it could only be myth that the railway from the post-independence era continues to bear fruits to India and helped the country to grow in stature.

The glorified side of the colonial railways in terms of development and constructing a national unity thrashed down to a minimal and became quite ominous for the peace of the country. It was during the partition in 1947 that the railways witnessed the human brutality and mass killing. The trains were the sole carrier of huge number of peoples from one side of the country to the other side of the country and while crossing the borders of newly formed India and Pakistan, those trains were attacked over religious animosity. Hundreds of people were killed in those partition trains. One of the most notable partition writers, Kushwant Singh, in his work *Train to Pakistan,* shared such horrific accounts of the partition. Suddenly, the angelic peace bearer tool of the colonialists took the image of blood trains loaded with corpses. The partition situation became a kind of a myth buster for the Indian people. Before the partition the trains were source of happiness and much glee for the Indian masses. The approaching and departure of trains were used to be considered as a source of much amusement, but the partition situation at the end of colonial rule forced the railways to be imagined as a blood train or a human killing machine. In popular imagination of the country, the trains were suddenly compared with mythical creatures of ominous breed. The trains were now considered as *Yamdut* who according to the Hindu religious belief was the spirit who carried away the dead person's soul either to heaven or hell. Such mythical formation of railways made the partition ambience much gloomier.

However, it needed to be remembered that the partition of 1947 was the direct outcome of religious animosity and intolerance between the two gigantic faith; Hinduism and Muslim. Their clash was the primary reason behind such bloodshed and hatred. It was their religious hatred that incurred so many deaths. The trains played no part at all in the bloodshed; trains were not the reason behind such bloodshed. Hence, it would be a complete mythical misrepresentation of the trains as blood trains or evil spirit bringing death and destruction. The trains were only used as carriers of huge masses and hence should not really affect the bloodshed by any means. But in popular partition literature, the imagery of trains was of evil in nature. Many partition narratives focused upon the gloomier aspect of the train. However, literature produced during the colonial period very often used the train's positive aspects of bringing equality and developing the nation by its existence and working in the transportation field. From Rudyard Kipling to Ruskin Bond, the railways always had a fascinating tale to be told.

At last but not least, the railways in folktales or in some other oral narratives always had a fascinating aspect of amusement associated with it. There had been numerous amounts of oral narratives existing in India from the Colonial period about the experiences of railway travel and the various kinds of adventure associated with it. In popular oral narratives, the trains were something of a supernatural creature driving away so many people at once with ridiculous amount of speed and efficiency. The rhythmical sound of the running of trains always attracted the tiny Indian masses to gaze at it like a Leviathan wondering in the fields and forests. The ignorant Indian masses that would travel by the train for the first time would give it a mythical kind of representation in his experiences and would also claim it to be a living organism of a spiritual kind. The journey through railways was always amusing with little blemishes every here and there, facing discrepancies at the hands of the colonial railway management authorities. Nonetheless, the tiny Indian masses never failed to look upon the railways as a petty spectator wondering about the working mechanism of such a magnificent innovation of science.

It is important to mention here that there was not one myth about the railways only but myths about the railways working prowess and management in colonial India. At the very beginning of the railways, when the railways were started to be established in India, it was seen as a fortunate opportunity for the Indian people to work and cooperate in such a gigantic project. However, little did they knew, that the Britishers were employing them with a very minimal and underpaid basis to work for them. The Britishers even tried to gather lands for railways construction by luring the landowners to donate their land for the development of the nation. That was completely a myth because the Britishers had not enough money to purchase such huge amount of lands and for their benefit they needed to lure such landowners into donating their land. The Britishers also lured several Indian investors to invest huge sum of money in such a project which was primarily designed for their own profit. The Britishers spread that myth in such a way that the gullible Indian masses were lured easily and befooled by them. It was also a myth that the railways or the private companies managing the railways had no such notion of profit seeking rather they tried to make the Indians believe that they were only working for the development of the Indian nation and trying to set the railways for the better management of the population density in India in terms of transportation.

To conclude, it could be safely said that the railways was a myth during its establishment in India because there were several difficulties in constructing the railways. Land, workers, construction material and huge amount of money was needed to be invested from the investors to make it possible to establish railways in India. It was so difficult to gather such a huge sum of money that lot of the foreign officials thought it was not possible to establish railways in such a populated density in India during the 1850's. The situation in India was very unlike the situation in England and even the weather in India was a great obstacle in constructing the railways in India. Hence, a huge number of men believed that the wish to establish a railway would only be a myth in India. But the cunningness of the Britishers and the gullibility of the Indians made it possible to establish the railways in India.

Thus, it could be said that the railways in colonial India was not only seen as a mythical representation but also seen as a myth within its own parameter of working. The railways which was previously thought to be a myth in Indian context became true and appeared with a handful scale of positivity for the Indian masses. However, the considered gift from Britain to India soon turned out to be a capitalist tool to maximize their profit and utilising the Indian resources like never before. The railways only helped the colonial rulers during the whole later half of the nineteenth century. It never failed to provide profit to such investors and private companies. The myth of establishing equality through railways became quite evident during the First World War and it broke down even severely during the partition. It was expected by many that the railways would bring a social equality and bonding among different classes, castes and religions in India but it was seen that it only furthered the cause even more severely. The divided bogies and class in the train always suggested a separation of people according to their ability to afford tickets. The division on such monetary ground was not the only thing, the Britishers always considered themselves superior from the general Indian masses and it was that sense of superiority that separated them from connecting with the Indian people. In several travel experiences in first class compartments, it was observed that Indians were humiliated for their ethnicity and habits. Discrepancies against the Indian passengers were many in numbers as against the discrepancies or issues faced by the white colonial masters. The racial division became even more severe in the railways during the colonial period. The necessary amenities such as drinking water and clean seating space were also limited with the first class passengers only. Most of Indians had to travel through the third class or second class compartments even if they could afford the railway fare. The numbers of outrages caused against the Indian women were endless. Thus, the railways became quite pathetic and dull in terms of the development of the society towards equality. Hence, it could be said that the colonial railways was a complete myth in terms of bringing social harmony. Thus, we could always say that, the colonial railways was considered to be promising but sadly it ended up being disclosed as a colonial scam which looked forward to loot the Indian resources and send them to Britain. Notable speaker Shashi Tharoor in one of his speeches delivered in Britain, explained the fact that how the railways were responsible for bringing down the GDP of the country in such a rapid pace. Thus, we could observe that the railways though played and had been playing a crucial part in terms of development of the country in the present day, it was not the same during the colonial phase and hence the railways which was considered a gift from Britain to India was nothing but a myth and a colonial scam.

Work Cited

Aguiar, Marian. *Tracking Modernity: India's Railway and the Culture of Mobility*. U of Minnesota P, 2011.

Awasthi, Aruna. *Railways and Cultural History: A Study of Poetic Representations*. Proceedings of the Indian History Congress, vol. 72, no.1, 2011, pp. 955-967.

Bear, Laura, Charlotte. *Traveling Modernity: Capitalism, Community and Nation in the Colonial Governance of the Indian Railways*. U of Michigan, 1998.

Bogart, Dan and Latika Chaudhary. *Railways in Colonial India: A New Economic History of Colonial India*. Routledge, 2015.

Chatterjee, Arup, K. *The Great Indian Railways: A Cultural Biography*. Bloomsbury Publishing, 2019.

Kerr, Ian, J. *Railways in Modern India*. Oxford UP, 2001.

Chaudhary, Latika, at el. *A New Economic History of Colonial India*. Routledge, 2015.

Mukhopadhyay, Aparajita. *Imperial Technology and 'Native' Agency: A Social History of Railways in Colonial India 1850-1920*. Taylor & Francis, 2018.

Chapter 15

Immortalising Myth through Language and Life

Suneela Sharma

Introduction

When we attempt to define myth, we embark upon different perspectives from which this word or phenomenon can be understood. The word 'myth' has etymological root in the Greek word 'mythos' and Latin word, 'mythus', meaning story, speech, thought, word, discourse, saga or tale-anything delivered by word of mouth . Myths, as a matter of fact, are stories about divine beings generally arranged in a coherent system; they are endorsed by rulers and priests, and are closely linked to religion'. (J.Simpson and S.Roud, 'Dictionary of English Folklore' 254.)

According to Merrasm Webster, myths are usually traditional stories of ostensibly historical events that serve to unfold a part of the world view of a group of people or explain a practice or belief of those people, or natural phenomenon related to the specific area of those people.

The Swiss psychoanalyst Carl Jung associated myth with collective unconscious that enabled him to regard the foundation of mythical images as positive and creative. Jung evolved a theory of archetypes. Broadly similar images and symbols occur in myths, fairy tales, and dreams because the human psyche has an inbuilt tendency to dwell on certain inherited motifs (archetypes), the basic pattern of which persists, however details may vary. Going by the above definitions , a myth has essential qualifications of being a "traditional" story, one that has proved of so lasting a value that it is continually retold, through whatever medium the artist/storyteller chooses to employ and therefore, embeds itself permanently in humanity's collective psyche.

Distinctions are often made between "myth," "saga" or "legend," and "folktale." A saga or legend is a story containing a kernel of historical truth, despite later fictional accretions whereas a folktale is a story of oral origin containing elements of fantasy or adventure of a hero or a heroine. While the main function of a saga or legend is to inspire or educate; a folktale aims at both entertainment and education with all sorts of insights. Under this rubric may be classed fairytales which are full of supernatural beings and magic and provide a more pointed moral content. Mythology, then, is the body of stories associated with a particular culture or institution or person. It is the corpus made up of the narratives and interpretations of these tales, stories and legends, all providing us a unique concept of life and world view.

Another perspective with which we can define myth and mythology is from the perspective of 'myth verses truth'. The line of this observation can be based on the fact that some real event or true story of the present times shall one day become a myth like the myths of today may have been the true happenings of the times long gone by. The literature comprising the epics of Homer's *Iliad*, *Odysseus* or Valmiki's *Ramayana* or, for that matter, Ved Vyasa's *Mahabharata* may seem to lack sufficient authentic evidences and proofs but we cannot deny their reality in the way they have become the warp and weft of the culture and people who have inherited them. This perspective or theory finds strength in the fact that the advance in technology today has identified enough evidences to authenticate several myths as the historical truths today. A famous example is that of the satellite picture confirming the existence of the famous *Ram Setu*, the bridge built by lord Rama's army to connect Indian sub-continent to the island of Sri Lanka in order to rescue his wife Sita from the captivity of Ravana, the king of Lanka, as mentioned in the epic of *Ramayana*. Another example is of the city of Troy which is the axis location of the *Iliad* and was for a long time considered to be a myth until Henerich Schliemann discovered the actual site and elevated the myth of Troy to the truth. Similarly Dwarika, a prominent location in the mythological epic of *Mahabharata* was discovered submerged under Arabian Sea in the current century. Therefore, in today's age the gap between myth and truth is constantly narrowing down.

Immortalising Myth and Myhtology

Myth and mythology are immortalised when they become a part and parcel of our language and life. Having stated this, we now have to initiate the inquiry of the current paper into the working of the above statement. The journey of the myths and mythologies from being narratives to becoming an indistinguishable and permanent part of language and culture of their inheritors is an intriguing one. Myths, as discussed above, are the stories of great events that happened in the lives of great men and women centuries ago. These stories may be true or fictional and their authenticity may lack solid proof at times. Myth and mythology, whether they have Greek, Biblical, Islamic, Oriental or Hindu origin, were initially passed on from one generation to the other over ages in the form of oral narrative, music, paintings, sculpture and literature. These stories got religious, moral or idealistic values and sanctions attached to them and their characters too became archetypes and metaphors representing all kinds of human qualities – the good, the evil, the bad or the ugly. The subsequent outcome of the tradition of orality was that not only were the mythological stories preserved as a corpus of literature, the characters of these stories too lived on as ideals, archetypes, metaphors, motifs, symbols and idioms in the communities inheriting them. They became part and parcel of the colloquial language, the language of daily use and gradually came to be even employed as literary devices in the literature. Although mythology may be a result of a purely instinctive and psychological human tendency to preserve the stories of past, through their prolonged use as metaphors and references they became role models, images or stereotypes of socio-cultural tradition, conduct and behaviour. Interestingly and strangely so, having traversed through centuries of its narration, a myth, in spite of becoming an integral part of a language and a culture, retains its own unique age-old existence, character, context, socio-cultural milieu, its own world-view and, therefore, gets immortalised.

To understand the phenomenon of immortalisation of myth through language use, we have chosen to study the two languages of Hindi and English. This shall be done by: first, identifying the various mythological references that have become a permanent component of these languages in Indian sub-continent, second, tracing the origins in the history or the narratives in which they are embedded, and third, trying to analyse their current status by connecting them to their current use vis-a-vis their life in the multi-lingual world of tomorrow.

Myth in Hindi Literature and Language

When we take up the corpus of Hindi language and literature, it lacks its luster bereft of the elements of epics of *Ramayana*, *Mahabharata* and the various narratives of *Puranas*. Whether it is the poetry of *Bhakti* movement, the age of Shamal Bhatt and Mir Taqi Mir in 18thcentury, the era of Rabindra Nath Tagore, Mirza Ghalib or Savitri Bai Phule, Bankim Chandra Chattopadhyaye in 19th century or the modern literature of the likes of U. R. Anantha Murthy, Suryakant Tripathi Nirala, Mahashweta Devi, Harishankar Parsai, literature of every age contextualises itself through the references of mythological incidents and characters.

A list of the mythological metaphors, stereotypes and archetypes that are popular in Hindi literature and are commonly used by the speakers speaking Hindi, follows here. The researcher of current paper herself is a user of Hindi as her mother tongue and the examples picked up are from her lifetime experience as a member of the community using the examples. Some of the most frequently used mythological metaphors and archetypes are explained for a better understanding of Indian myths and legends.

Narada is believed to be one of the sons of Brahma, the mythological creator of the universe as referred in *Puranas*. His image is of a musical and a storyteller sage carrying musical instruments *khartal* and a *veena*. The mythological epic stories of *Ramayana, Mahabharata* and many other texts paint him in the role of a cursed travelling messenger of God who would travel to distant worlds and realms referred to as *Lokas* sharing the information about the incidents of one world with the other world. At the same time, no one would believe in him because of the curse. There are many humorous tales that depict Narada as a wise but mischievous character announcing his entry at a place by chanting *Narayana, Narayana* (the name of another God Vishnu).The metaphor *'Naradmuni'* is frequently used in Indian households for gossip mongers and rumour mongers.

Goddess Lakshmi is one of the most popular female mythological characters who hails from the famous epic story of the

Churning of the Ocean or *Sagar Manthan*. She symbolises beauty, fertility and abundance by the sheer image that she portrays. She is shown sitting on a lotus flower with four arms, a lotus in each of his raised two upper hands, with gold coins falling from the palms of the two lower hands. The metaphor of *Laxmi* is ardently used for girls in Indian households at the time of their birth or wedding.

From the Hindu mythological age called *Treta Yuga* of the epic story of the *Ramayana*, there are several examples of archetypal found and used in Hindi language in Indian households even today. Lord Rama, the king of *Ayodhya*, is an extremely popular metaphor of an ideal man – the *Maryada Purush* who epitomises the qualities of courage, wisdom, character and strength. *Ram Rajya* is the archetype world-view of the ideal nation popularly used by Indians both in Hindi and in English. The concept contextualises itself in the ideal administration run by Lord Rama in his kingdom of *Ayodhya*. At the same time, the archetype of *Sone ki Lanka* or the Lanka made of Gold is popularly used as a proverb in Hindi language to convey the message of futility of the golden splendour of Ravana's power, his Lanka was reduced to ashes when Hanuman burnt it with his tail set ablaze. Hanuman is another frequently used archetypal character who stands for loyalty. The examples of Hanuman's undaunted loyalty in travelling to Sri Lanka to bring the news of Lord Rama's wife Sita for him and later bringing a rare herb to revive Lakshmana, Rama's brother's life, are known to every child in every Indian household through the use of such references as a daily religious ritual. Another very popular character from the epic of *Ramayana* is Manthra the archetype of evil. The character happens to be the royal attendant of Lord Rama's stepmother Kaikeyi and plays a negative role in sending off the two brothers Rama and Lakshmana to exile and establishing Kaikeyi's son Bharat as the King of Ayodhya. Another popular proverb derived from *Ramayana* of household use is *Ghar Ka Bhedi Lanka Dhaye* which signifies the role played by Vibheeshan, Ravana's brother, in his downfall by revealing to Rama the secret of the life source in the navel of his brother. Similarly, there are several archetypes and metaphors found in Hindi language from *Mahabharata* that seemed to have occurred during the iconic *Dwapar Yuga*. Some very popular characters and references are as follows.

Lord Krishna is one of the most favourite and famous archetypal Hindu mythological characters. The multiple images belonging to the various stages of his life carry different archetypes with them. His image of a child stealing butter or playing mischievous frolic with the shepherd girls of Vrindavan in waters of Gomti river present him as a prankster. There is an image of Krishna holding flute to his lips with both hands, standing with legs crossed, adorned with bright royal attire and ornaments with his consort Radha clinging to him is an image representing celebration of tenderness, love and life. At a later stage in his life, his image as the charioteer of Arjuna during the battle of Kurukshetra, presents him as a divine master and guide teaching the life skills of *Bhagwad Gita*.

Another character from the epic of *Mahabharata* is an all-time favorite archetypal of an evil maternal uncle in Indian households. This character plays a negative role in hatching conspiracies against Pandava brothers, resulting in their defeat in the game of dice, stripping their wife Draupadi off her saree in public and subsequent exile of Pandavas.

Kansa plays a negative role in the *Bhagwad Purana* by trying to kill lord Krishna, the son of his own sister Devki, in fear of his own death at the hands of his nephew, as per the prophecy. The example of the love and bond of friendship between Sudaama, a poor Brahmin and Krishna, a king, from *Bhagwad Purana* is used as an archetype of true friendship.

Apart from these two epics there are several mythological stories of commoners, heroes, kings, fables and folklores the likes of 'Savitri and Satyavan' from where the metaphoric phrase of *Sati Savitri* – the epitome of a wife's loyalty for husband has emerged as Hindi idiomatic phrase. Similarly the metaphor of *Satyavaadi Harishchandra* has its roots in the story of *Raja Harishchandra* who once lost all his family, throne, belongings and life because he was truthful. Shravan Kumar is one role model whose reference as a metaphor of love for parents is a proverbial part of Hindi language. The list of such examples is endless but the ones identified above are the most frequently used and accepted examples of mythological metaphors and archetypes that have become living entities in Hindi language.

It becomes imperative here to study the examples of the metaphors and archetypes of the mythological characters found in the English language as well for a better understanding of myths of different continents and their mythological relevance in their lives.

The tales of Greek gods, goddesses, kings, and heroes survived for thousands of years, dominated the Biblical era and even today they are more talked about than any of the Egyptian, Roman or Chinese Gods in the world. Some of the archetype metaphors, idiomatic phrases and proverbs are identified and analysed below.

Zues is the God of sky, lightning and thunder and rules the gods on Mount Olympus, the reference of which in literature of all times has preserved itself. This archetype is a judge-like character, answerable only to himself and responsible for overall order. At times the perfection is double edged with Zeus referred to as a symbol of tyrannical behaviour willing to indulge in his own vices and is often used as a patriarchal archetypal in current English language.

Aphrodite is Greek Goddess of love, passion, pleasure, female beauty and procreation. Aphrodite archetypal is the symbol of all embodiments of love–sensual, sexual, maternal and companionship, and reigns supreme among the popular English metaphors.

The archetypal of Apollo, the God of healing, medicine, archery, music and poetry, is a mythological character and is the most popularly used metaphor of an ideal man in English literature and language of common usage. There are several gods and goddesses who are more popular as the metaphoric archetypal amongst the native users of English and these are – Athena, Hermes, Poseidon, Hades, Persephone and Dionysus, Aphrodite, Osiris. In fact, the modern English language has a profuse presence of Greek mythological element in the form character archetypes, idiomatic and proverbial archetypes. A very popular idiom – 'to open a Pandora's box' has its context in Greek mythology. When Prometheus stole the fire from heaven, Zeus the king of Gods, took vengeance by presenting Pandora to Epimetheus, the brother of Prometheus. Pandora released all the sickness and death into the world when she opened a jar that was given to her by Zeus. Therefore, in modern day English the idiom–to open a Pandora's box means to start something that will have many troublesome consequences.

Then there are Greek heroes of the great epic of Trojan War form the magnificent 'Iliad' of Homer. There are heroes and warriors of the stature of Hercules, Achilles, Peruses, Theses, Odysseus, Atlas, Orpheus, Agamemnon, Adonis, Actaeon, etc.

Hercules is an archetype hero possessing all the qualities of courage, valour, strength, passion, outstanding achievements and noble qualities. A born Demi-God, the son of Zeus, brave and powerful Hercules is perhaps the most loved of Greek heroes and, therefore, any work of impossible nature is referred to as Herculean in nature in the modern English of today.

Achilles heel is a striking archetype of a Greek hero who fights wars, worships Gods and understands his role in the divine scheme of events. In the epic of Trojan war, Achilles plays the god like hero with passions bowing down before the divine command to "check your rage". As an infant Achilles' mother dipped him into the river Styx which made him vulnerable everywhere but in his heels. Therefore, the phrase Achilles' heel means weakness in spite of an overall strength that leads to one's downfall.

Odysseus is another most favourite of the Greek warriors, the king of Ithaca who fought relentlessly throughout the Trojan War till they won. An archetype of extremely difficult situation is often called an Odyssey which incidentally, is the name of the book of the tales of Odysseus's bravery.

In Greek mythology, Adonis, a shepherd boy, who represented youth, beauty and desire, the mortal lover of the Goddess Aphrodite, was considered one of the most handsome men of ancient Greece, so attractive in fact, his name became a metaphor for male physical beauty.

Oedipus is a tragic character from Greek mythology who fulfils a prophecy when he unintentionally kills his father Laius and marries his mother, Jocasta, bringing catastrophe and misery upon his city and family. Oedipus is the subject of a Greek tragedy; Oedipus Rex, written by ancient Greek playwright Sophocles. The Oedipus Complex, is a concept, introduced in 1899 by psychoanalyst Sigmund Freud.

Some more phrases that are popularly used in modern day English are discussed here.

Touch wood: The habit of knocking on, or touching wood to avoid tempting fate or to bring good luck goes way back thousands of years, to ancient Greece where it was believed that lived inside trees.

The Midas Touch: We refer to someone who has great success in financial dealings, someone who succeeds in anything he puts his hand to as having a *'Midas Touch'*. The phrase comes from the Greek myth about Midas, the greedy king of Phrygia, in Asia Minor, who was granted a wish by Dionysus, God of the harvest. Midas wished for everything he touched, to turn to gold, if only he had given more thought to his wish. Literally, everything he touched, turned to solid gold, food, wine, and most sadly of all, his precious daughter Zoe.

Biblical Archetypes and Metaphors in English

A few centuries later, Bible and Christianity revived the story of the Genesis, the grand epic story of the creation of Man and Woman and their subsequent fall from Paradise because of Satan and his conspiracies to thwart the Divine will of God. There are several archetypal characters of Bible that were employed age after age by literary artists of English literature. Today they have become a part and parcel of English language and its world view. Some of them are discussed below.

Three major archetypes of Bible are the concepts of Paradise, the Tree of knowledge and the Tree of Life. Paradise is an archetype of a perfect world in perfect harmony. The two trees in the Paradise, the *Tree of Knowledge* andthe *Tree of Life* are the archetypes of the idea of the knowledge being a precursor of sin and temporariness of good because of evil in our lives. The archetype of paradise represents perfection and a return to it signifies a utopia.

The snake or serpent from the story of Genesis has become a popular archetype or metaphor for temptation and evil and symbolises human instinct to be lured by sensual or carnal temptation. Satan takes the shape of a serpent in the Garden of Eden and entices Eve to eat the fruit of the tree of knowledge. The use of these metaphors is very frequent by the native speakers of English all over the world.

Some more very popular biblical proverbs and phrases are:

'Damsel in Distress' is taken from the story of Ruth. Ruth is an archetype of a woman in serious circumstances who needs a hero to come to her rescue. She goes with Naomi to Bethlehem and picks barley from the fields owned by Naomi's relative Boaz who then marries her.

'Carrying one's Cross' is from Bible and refers to Jesus carrying a cross that has come to be symbolic of the world's problems. Therefore, when people are told to carry their own cross they are told to deal with their own burdens.

'At your wit's end' has its earliest reference in English to the late 14th century. The phrase comes from Psalm 107, in which "they that go down to the sea in ships, they reel to and fro, and stagger like a drunken man, and are at their wit's end" (107: 23-27).

'Eat, drink and be merry' is another popular sentiment which is outlined several times in Bible (Luke 12:19, 1 Corinthians 15:32), but appears first in the Book of Ecclesiastes: "man hath no better thing under the sun, than to eat, and to drink, and to be merry" (8:15).

The phrase 'feet of clay' phrase refers to a fundamental weakness that has the potential to lead to the downfall of something (or someone) otherwise great and powerful. It comes from the Book of Daniel (2:31-45)

'The land of milk and honey' is related to Exodus (3:1-22). Moses is told by the vision of the burning bush to lead the Israelites out of Egypt and into Canaan, 'a land flowing with milk and honey'. The phrase has since come to be widely used of any location promising great prosperity, respite, and comfort.

Thus, in all times to come these archetypes and metaphors were profusely used and exploited by the greatest of literary artists whether it was Shakespeare, Milton, Alexander Pope, Samuel Taylor Coleridge or the modernists like T. S. Eliot. In the contemporary English language we have countless mythological archetypes, metaphors, idioms, phrases and proverbs living through and enriching the English language.

After an in-depth study of the history of the mythological narratives and characters in the languages of Hindi and English and their current indisputable value in these languages today, we can safely conclude that about one fourth of the corpus of Hindi and English languages has been borrowed from myth and mythological narratives. Myth and mythological elements are the soul of the languages and cultures that have inherited them. Myth and mythology can be preserved through various other media like religion, paintings, music, folk songs etc. The literature of a language is the best mode to preserve the rich heritage of the mythology of a society. Language is still the best medium to keep the myth alive through their use as references, proverbs, metaphors and examples in real life situational and routine conversation. Myth can live eternally as long as it has language to carry it along.

Works Cited

https://www.merriam-webster.com/nodictionary/mythI.

https://global.oup.com/us/.

https://global.oup.com/us/companion.websites/.

https://en.wikiversity.org/wiki/Classical_Mythology/Jungian_psychology.

https://www.britannica.com/topic/myth/Myth-in-culture.

https://www.mentalfloss.com/article/61964/18-everyday-expressions-borrowed-biblesegal_jung on mythology.pdfg.

Chapter 16

Mythology of Witchcraft and Transgressive Femininity in Mainstream Movies *The Conjuring*, *The Love Witch*, and *Bulbbul*

Tanvi Punia

Oxford English Dictionary defines 'witch' as "a woman who is believed to have magic powers, especially to do evil things" (online). The figure of 'witch' has enjoyed much popularity from the public both in cinema and in other popular media. This figure of the witch has been appropriated by filmmakers in cinema not only to market fear and thrill in the audience but, at times, also to portray transgressive femininity on screen at its best. From the three witches of Macbeth to the witch Bathsheba of *The Conjuring*, the West has a very rich and fascinating history of witch hunts and supremacy. Shakespeare, in one of his most popular tragedies *Macbeth,* presented the three witches as figures not only of power but also of trickery, deception, and challenge. They are, the Bard of Avon says, "so withered, and so wild" and mysterious figures who destabilise the social, cultural, and political universe of the patriarchy and lead men to ruin and destruction (41).

English society began to see witchcraft differently and punish it harsher in the second part of the sixteenth century, as "a crime against God" (Robbins 161) similar to how the Catholic Inquisition had long viewed and perceived it on the Continent. According to estimations, at least "200,000 supposed witches were put to death in Europe during the witch hunt between the fifteenth and eighteenth centuries, and many more badly tortured, all in the name of the Christian Church" (Moore 141). "It would be hard to find a woman who is neither a bitch nor a ninny – if so, she will be a witch and fey," wrote the 19th century French writer Louis Ferdinand Destouches aka Céline to Milton Hindus (…..).

Since time immemorial, women have been expected to live their lives by the norms dictated by patriarchy and whenever any woman took the reins of her life into her hands, the fear of female liberation and sexuality pushed society to brand her as a 'witch' to ostracize her from the mainstream society. Demands were raised to 'burn the witch' as a warning so that no woman dares to transgress further. Nonetheless, women across centuries have often resorted to witchcraft to 'get what they want' or often just their transgressive activities have earned them the tag of a *witch*, *chudail*, or *daayan*. Fear of female sexuality led men to burn the witches at stake as they were afraid of the emotions they elicited in them. Witches identified their sexuality as the most powerful weapon to control men and to get what they want. They made magic potions with hallucinogenic herbs and had the power to curse and ruin people. Witches were also accused of damaging harvests and cattle, spreading diseases, eating up children and stealing penises of men, rumours which helped men to destroy the witches. Men have always feared powerful women and witches have often been compared with the feminists by scholars.

Witchcraft has a wide range of meanings since the idea is so adaptable. Wicca is a recognised religion and its followers are identified as 'witches' Witch and witchcraft are common themes in children literature, horror movies, and newspaper cartoons because they all share similar concepts and symbolism. Even minor conflicts and injustices are frequently decried as witch-hunts, and the term 'witch' is still used to disparage women. Even individuals who have relegated witchcraft to history's trash bin along with other remnants of primitivism are culturally resilient, pertinent, and powerful beings. The witches are unique. Although Quakers, Cathars, and Lollards were all persecuted, it is difficult to envision a board game on them. Why? They had little mystery about them since they lived firmly and solely in the natural world. However, witches irritate the unconscious.

The theism, animism, and conflict, along with the legalism that defined cursing so as to better proscribe and punish it, are consequently the fundamental components of witchcraft that may be found in the oldest civilisation. In Egypt, not much has changed either. Taboos, rituals, and spells were pervasive, and the open border between this world and the next was intricately built. Rome and Greece adopted the Egyptian model. The classical civilisation was steeped in the dark manipulation of spirits despite its grandeur and majesty; this provided a way to sooth tension, channel rage, and satiate desire. This was neither a forerunner of the arts and sciences that the rising West would later praise, nor was it aberrant or residual. Everyone's culture and mindset included magic as a vital and accepted aspect of reality. We should take the good with the bad, or the superstitious with the rational while studying the social history of the ancients.

There were numerous different witchcraft mythologies prevalent in the fifteenth century. In some regions, these mythologies persisted for many years, retaining their distinctive features with surprising persistence. The one mythology of witchcraft is explained by assigning its beginnings to mediaeval heresies, ritual magic, the stubborn European peasant culture, or Christians' attempts to strengthen their own shaky faith by searching for supernatural proof. The components of witchcraft soon solidified into that cumulative construct, into a notion of "the Sabbath," which develops very early in the fourteenth century through the agglutination of components in a single mythology. This is a point on which historians of many arguments may concur. Although this is accurate, significant, and more evident than any of us understood before, the point is not only that there are many geographical variations of witchcraft mythologies and that they are plural rather than singular.

The first movie that I examine to understand the politics of the representation of witches on the screen is *The Conjuring*. *The Conjuring* is a 2013 American supernatural horror film directed by James Wan and written by Chad Hayes and Carey W. Hayes. This is one of the most popular movies in Hollywood centering on the alleged real-life exploits of Ed and Lorraine Warren, a married couple who investigated paranormal events. *The Conjuring,* which is set in 1971, revolves around a purportedly real-life witch Bathsheba Sherman. *The Conjuring* tells the story of the Perron family, mother, father, and four girls who move out to a house in the country, far and away from the civilisation in the middle of nowhere. Soon enough, they discover a mysterious boarded-up basement in their house and a standard possession-haunting scenario develops, with flying pictures, creepy sleepwalking, terrifying apparitions and night screams and hysterical laughter and shouts. Coming to their aid are the Warrens, a husband-and-wife team of ghost busting paranormal experts, with Ed Warren, playing the academic, and his wife, the strong-willed psychic.

This movie is much feminist in its approach and presents both the witch and the female paranormal investigator Lorraine as equally powerful figures. The witch Bathsheba that constitutes the main antagonist is indeed a descendant of a Salem witch. In the movie, Bathsheba, the witch who possesses mothers to kill children, is a terrifying figure who has terrorised generations and is much daunted the Church as well. The Church actually plays an idle role in the movie. Even Ed's exorcism fails to suppress Bathsheba, the witch.

This successfully shows why patriarchy stigmatises witches. It is simply because they cannot control these powerful men and are scared of their power. In fact, every traditional male institution in the film can only stand idle while the women steal the scene. The Vatican, though treated as the supreme solution, plays only an obstructive role. The terms 'women' and 'power' are paradoxical in patriarchal vocabulary and the witches strongly subvert this established power structure. In *The Conjuring* also, Bathsheba is presented as a power-hungry woman who sacrificed her child to Satan for immortality and thereafter hung herself from a tree near her house when caught red-handedly by her husband later. Here, the politics of representation of witches always as the 'evil other' on the screen is fascinating. The horror movies that centre on witches always come up with manipulative stories mostly to project the women with power as "baddies."

In the popular imagination, a woman is generally thought of as a mother, daughter, sister or friend. A woman is mostly seen as a nurturing and caring figure that gives birth and sustains life. Witches, on the other hand, hammer these stereotypical roles of women and emerge as all-destructive figures threatening the male hegemony of the patriarchal society. Witches in Hollywood movies are always portrayed as a threat to the patricentric Roman Catholic Church. Even if the witches are presented as subversive figures of power, they are also shown to be suppressed by the Father or the male priest of the church who makes her surrender to the Holy Trinity, which, though a holy power, also ironically symbolises the patriarchal hegemony and control. For decades now, filmmakers have appropriated the figure of the witches in popular horror cinema not only to thrill and terrify the public but also to present a transgressive female figure who, though destroyed in the end, will still leave traces of her power.

Another movie that presents a subversive witch figure is *The Love Witch* which is a 2016 American comedy horror film written, edited, directed, produced, and scored by Anna Biller. *The Love Witch* presents a very unconventional witch figure. She does not look scary. She does not roam about the night sky in cone hats on brooms. In the movie, Elaine, a beautiful young woman is a witch who practices witchcraft as an alternate religion to get love. She is thirsty for love and applies witchcraft on men to make them fall in love with her and worship her as the ultimate fantasy. The protagonist is aware of the importance of female representation but believes that it must go beyond mere inclusion. Perspective and profundity are fundamental, and occasionally it takes the "wrong" kind of woman to show how harmful patriarchal preconceptions of women can be. The presence of female villain-protagonists inherently subverts a genre that has long seen female, puritan protagonists from the perspective of male directors. The creation of truly original movies like *The Love Witch* in the twenty-first century is made possible by feminist filmmakers like Anna Biller, who are distinctive in their style and subject matter.

Till now, I have discussed the white or the First-World witches only. But now, I will also discuss the Third-World witches. In this context, I explore the scenario of the witches in our country, India. India is a very superstitious country in these respects and has a rich history surrounding witches. In India also, women for centuries have practiced black magic and witchcraft. Witchcraft cults, which were previously prevalent in native tribal groups, are now obscure and minor. Witchcraft may be seen as a female uprising against the existing social order and authorities, as well as a male uprising against women to establish the order that men want to see in society. But here, I will take a different turn and explore what it means to be a witch in the eyes of a conservative society. Does a woman need to have supernatural powers to be called a witch? Or just a voice of protest from her is enough to ostracize her as a witch? What does the term 'witch' mean? What connotations does it have in the popular imagination? Does being a witch necessarily mean knowledge of witchcraft or is any transgressive woman prone to being called a witch?

At this point I would like to take into account the movie *Bulbbul* by Anvita Dutt. The movie is set in the 19th-century Bengal Presidency in British India. As the movie opens, we see a 5-year-old Bulbbul getting married to a middle-aged zamindar. From the very beginning, the movie hints at the 'control' imposed on women by various institutions, marriage in particular, and patriarchy in general.

19th century Bengal was a place of superstitions and conservatism, like any other place in India, where speaking or protesting of women was deemed abnormal. The movie next fast forwards to 20 years later when Satya, the zamindar's brother and Bulbbul's childhood companion returns from London after 5 years on completion of his studies. As he returns, he is told about the *Chudail* who haunts his village and kills men every night. He goes out on hunts to catch the *Chudail* but fails to do so. Meanwhile, he also notices the changes in Bulbbul in these 5 years. She is no longer the innocent, simple girl that she used to be but an indifferent, daring, and courageous girl. Blood moon and red light are constant motifs in the movie which foreground the blood spilled of people throughout the movie. In flashback, we are shown how Bulbbul and Satya came closer since their childhood days and gradually how Bulbbul started loving him.

This movie is a social commentary on many social evils like child marriage, domestic abuse, and the superstitions and prejudices which ruin the lives of many innocent women. As the movie progresses, we find out that, after knowing that Bulbbul loves his brother and not him, Bulbbul's husband beats her mercilessly and leaves her crippled. Her feet become twisted and she is further raped by another brother-in-law who was supposedly insane. These incidents erase all her innocence and make her ferocious. Since then, every night she goes out with her twisted feet to kill men who abuse their wives or any woman. At every crime scene, the blood prints of the twisted feet made the villagers believe that it was nothing but the workings of a witch.

Thus, here we see that a woman does not necessarily need to have supernatural powers to be called a witch. It is just the circumstances and the activities that make a woman a witch in the eyes of the society. Being called a witch at times is only about the boundaries you cross and the transgressions you make.

Therefore, I would like to conclude that the idea of the witch is more of a social construct than anything real. It just reflects the fear of patriarchy from the powerful women. Portrayal of witches on screen also, in this regard, does not just market fear, it portrays fearless powerful women who do not bow down to the social system and who also unleash vengeance for every wrong committed against them. Even the movies I have referred to also reflect the pro-feminist stance of the movies where witches are considered as the ultimate feminists.

Works Cited

Biller, Anna, Director. *The Love Witch*. Oscilloscope, 2016. Prime Video, https://www.primevideo.com/detail/The-Love-Witch/0SXI7W2K4A2A SMZTUXI I8QT.

Guptan, Anvita Dutt, Director. *Bulbbul.* Clean Slate Filmz, 2020. Netflix, https://www.netflix.com/title/81029150.

Hindus, Milton. *Céline: The Crippled Giant.* Routledge, 2020.

Moore, Mavor. *Shakespeare and Witchcraft: Stratford Papers on Shakespeare.* Editor B.W. Jackson.W.J. Gage, 1962.

Robbins, Rossell Hope. *The Encyclopedia of Witchcraft and Demonology*. Crown Publishers, 1959.

Shakespeare, William. *Macbeth*. Wordsworth Classics, 1992.

The Oxford English Dictionary. 2nd ed. 1989.OED Online. Accessed 2 Jan. 2023.

Wan, James, Director. *The Conjuring.* Warner Bros. Pictures, 2013. Netflix, https://www.netflix.com/title/70251894.

Chapter 17

Performative, Performance and Retold Myths in Poile Sengupta's *Thus Spake Shoorpanakha, So Said Shakuni*

Sanjeev Kumar

A play is a performance in a specific space. Contemporary theorists, critics and scholars, especially those practicing Performance Theory, assume stage to be a fictional space. They also maintain that in a proper understanding of the play being performed, the distance between the audience and the actors poses additional problems because of the fact that there is direct transfer from real-life interaction with people around us to the actors on the stage (Fludernick 22). This brings in the question of performance of the actors on the stage and those sitting and watching the play as audience. The success and failure of the actors to communicate the written words and ideas to the audience essentially depends on the people as spectators as they attempt to connect with performed ideas to their own ideas and frame of mind leading, thus, to their agreement or disagreement which, as a matter of fact, depends on their socio-cultural background.

A character on the stage, while performing, is also influenced by his "reconstruction of other character's mental models" and, as such, the "dramatic staples of manipulation, intrigue, mistaken identities, subterfuge and dramatic irony are founded upon the social nature of consciousness" (Zettelmann 54). Such a 'consciousness,' at times, restricts and restrains the actors to free himself from *it* and get connected to the spectators who, in term, have their own consciosnesses. The role of the spectators, in this sense, becomes significant as he has his own performance as a spectator. Zettelmann elaborates this phenomenon:

> Dramatic audiences perform astoundingly complex mental feats. Every major character is the bearer of his or her own individual possible world, his or her own model of the dramatic universe. It is the task of the audience to reconstruct the contents of each possible world on the basis of the entirety of semiotic data ascribed to that character (53-54).

Poile Sengupta is one of the few playwrights in contemporary India who deals with myths and through mythical characters attempts to highlight the marginalised characters and their pain and anguished which they suffered in mythological narratives. While explaining her take on theatre and plays writing, she says, "Theatre is performance.... It brings together, for a period of time, an audial and visual presentation of an idea or agenda, a given space, and an audience" (*India International*113). Theatre, for her, involves performative action and, through such actions, an idea is conveyed to the audience within a specific period of time. This paper studies her play *Thus Spake Shoorpanakha, So Said Shakuni* in the purview of the statement made by the playwright and to see as to what extent she addresses the contemporary issues through myths and how, through performative representation, they are eventually conveyed to the audience.

Thus Spake Shoorpanakha: So Said Shakuni shows how it feels to be a persona of wicked reputation while, outside the myth, he or she may be a being of affirmativequality. The question is how the readers or audience see that character on the written page or stage. The perception of the readers or audience, however, depends on their association with the socio-cultural background of what is being presented on the pages or stage. It is pertinent to mention here that, whether one knows it or not, his interpretation of thewritten word or stage performance is entirely dependent on his learning or knowledge of what is being presented by the playwright and the how of it.

Performance and representation, in fact, are complementary to each other. Performance is representation of the presentation–what is being presented by the playwright on the pages. Performance, in this nous, cannot be separated from presentation and representation. If there is any difference, it may be the variance of how the performance is being enacted on the stage. An understanding of what 'performance' means is imperative here. Performance, Richard Schechner argues, is the broadest yet "most ill-defined disc" and includes the "whole constellation of events, most of them passing unnoticed, that takes place in both performers and audience from the time the first spectator enters the field of performance – the precinct where the theatre takes place – to the time the last spectator leaves" (8). In the third issue of *The Drama Review* in 1988, Schechner maintains that performance "is a broad spectrum of activities, including at the very least the performing arts, rituals, healing, sports, popular entertainments, and performance in everyday life" (4).

Performance, as a matter of fact, includes all through which the presentation gets communicated to the audience. It is "showing doing," as Schechner finally asserts (*Performance Studies* 2), which requires people "to train for and rehearse their actions, and that this is true in everyday life every bit as much as it is art" (Reinelt 12). Drama Studies, writes Janelle Reinelt, however, began to treat "texts as performance texts; that is, as material for others, in rehearsal and performance, to produce as particular productions" (17). Graham Holderness explains this shift:

> There is virtually no focus on the dramatist, and no projected vision of a culture's ideological totality: the dramatic performance itself, conceived as the physical realisation of an enacted relationship with social convention, belief, and ideology, mediates between them (4).

Performance, thus, considers mankind essentially as performative beings. It is, Bert O. States opines, "strictly a metaphor for social behavior" (5).Performance, in fact, performs. Peggy Phelan argues, "Performance's only life is in the present. Performance cannot be saved, recorded, documented, or otherwise participate in the circulation of representations *of* representations: once it does so, it becomes something other than performance ... [it] becomes itself through disappearance" (146). Performance, thus, is transitive in nature.

Representation is both historically and theoretically essential to our ideological expression about literature and culture which, in terms, is connected with *mimesis* of Aristotle. It depends on context, intellectual discipline, and the bits and pieces of enquiry. Christopher Prendergast maintains that representation "is not linked to the principle of distortion but on the contrary to the idea of a fully accurate or faithful reflection of reality (4).This "constitutively depends on psychological intention, for whether one thing represents a second thing constitutively depends on whether a subject 'takes the first to represent the second' (Kalhat 19). In a dramatic representation, one must remember, the production and its understanding exploit the illusion that what (animate/inanimate) represents and what is represented remain indistinguishable/alike. Javier Kalhat expounds this make-believe representation:

> What is distinctive about the actor's representation ... is that, within the context of the theatrical performance, the actor is taken to be *make-believe identical* with ... [the character] .... Actors and audience collude to create and sustain the dramatic illusion ... and each party knows that the other knows that the whole thing is an elaborate game of make-believe. What holds for actors, also holds for sets, props, lighting, and any other representational device or mechanism that helps to create and sustain the dramatic illusion (22).

Representation in theatre, opines Belen Tortosa Pujante, has generally been understood as "a unique event originating in the simultaneous presence and mutual perception of a number ofactors and the audience attending a play" (156). This involves a concurrent assumption that in a play as performance "something necessarily *happens*" (Pujante 156). What *happens* is essentially related to the involvement of the people as audience who get associated to the play in some ways. This, however, may be challenged in contemporary theatre as, in Performance Theory, one may question such associations of the audience that, as a matter of fact, involve those who are sitting at home and watching the same performance on TV. Jacques Ranciere argues in this connection:

> What exactly occurs among theatre spectators that cannot happen anywhere? What is more interactive, more communitarian about these spectators than a mass of individuals watching the same television show at the same hour? (16).

Thus Spake Shoorpanakha, So Said Shakuni represents two characters who accomplish their two roles independently–one as a contemporary man and woman and the other as represented or misrepresented in two myths derived from two Indian epics – *Mahabharata* and *Ramayana*. The plot of the play is setin a swarming airport where the two characters, Man and Woman meet while waiting for a deferred flight. The two characters are "modern in their speech, attitude and behaviour," Sengupta asserts, and the play, "challenges the conventional vilification of Shoorpanakha and Shakuni and presents them differently, not only in the narrative but also in stage technique and structure" (*Women Centre Stage* 242). The play reveals that underneath the old-fashioned title, there is an emphasis on the contemporary subjects through merging of the stories from two dissimilar epics–*Mahabharata* and *Ramayana*.

In the opening of the play, the reader/audience finds that the airport is full of "highly inflammable people" who are waiting for the indefinitely postponed flights (*Thus Spake* 247). Soon enough one hears Woman saying, "to be a woman…to want a man so much that…that the rest of the world disappears" (*Thus Spake* 252). She recounts the incident and adds that "there they are in the forest living in a pretty cottage when this absolutely stunning woman comes along. The two brothers, especially the older one, is bowled over. Totally bowled over" (*Thus Spake* 254). Man in the play, fails to understand what was going on till Woman says, "It's my story…I was her" (*Thus Spake* 255). It is here that Man and the readers/audience come to know that she is Shoorpanakha who is retelling her tale of misery and how she was mistreated and made "the other woman" (*Thus Spake* 256). She describes the elder brother:

> He was the most desirable man I had ever seen and yet it was not his eyes or lips, or his fingers or his wide shoulders that took away…took away the breath in my throat. It was what happened to me in that instant. I wanted him to tear my clothes off and tear through me and yet I also wanted him to be tender and melting. I would suckle him (*Thus Spake* 256-57).

In the legendary story of *Ramayana,* it is here when Shoorpanakha gets bewitched with the vivacity of Ram and goes closer to him to express her love and longing for him. This was not a common act then, but in the contemporary world, a woman is accepted and admired to be straightforward and given respect for her unaffected thoughts and expression. Shoorpanakha was rejected, however, for the reason that Ram was already wedded and he asked her to go to Laxman and pursue his yes. She feels disgraced and expresses her annoyance and bitterness:

> You know what they did to me…the two brothers…they laughed. Laughed at me. They teased me. Mocked me. The older one said, ask my brother…he might want you…the younger one said…I can't marry without my brother's consent…ask him…They tossed me this way and that, as if…as if I did not deserve any more respect. As if I was a…a broken thing (*Thus Spake* 261).

The younger brother, Shoorpanakha agonisingly explains, chopped off whatever "stood out" from her, whatever "stuck out" – her breasts, her ears and her nose (*Thus Spake* 262). She breaks down and states:

> I was bleeding…all down my face…my chest…bleeding…Was it so wrong to tell a man 'I love you'?...I was wailing. I was raging, I was sobbing. I wanted to hit him…. I wanted to squeeze him. I wanted to lie

> under him and watch his face change...I wanted love...just a little love...for a little while (*Thus Spake* 262).

It is here that the audience feels analogous to her and feels compassion for her. This theatrical representation of myth is somewhat different from what exists in the epic *Ramayana.* It is here where we find the blending of fact and fiction. It is for this representation for performative act that the mythic story line is transformed and the audience feels fellow feeling as well as empathy for the character.

It would not be out of context to mention here that a play is written for performance, that is, a play is a drama that involves the impersonators and the assembled audience that hopes to be beguiled, stirred, amused, provoked or affected in some profound way by the spectacle created by a host of impersonators. In drama, first, there is obvious absence of the author from the play and, secondly, the presence of the stage/staging. This brings in the issue of truth and drama, as Roger Savage asks in this connection, "Is the performer's job to locate and communicate the author's central truth in a script, or to pursue and promote some truth of their own that work on it has led them to?" (163). Savage elaborates this:

> First and foremost that it is valuable to build a 'theatre of the imagination' in your mind, so that plays on the page can begin to generate the sort of life they have inherent in them. If that 'theatrical event bigger than the script' is not about to take place in the world outside you, let it happen in your head (166).

While the imaginative theatre flourishes in the mind of the readers, it is worthwhile to note here, they have to bear in mind the elements of pace, unstoppability, pre-thought-out characterization, stage-configuration, atmosphere and occasion related to that performance which help and enable them to imbibe certain free-from-author thoughts.

Poile Sengupta has been cognizant of the fact that "a play in the pages of a book is not a finished product (*India International* 116). She argues that the "acting area, however big or small it may be, however formal or informal, is, for a time, a sacred, creative space" where the characters enact their given roles that gets influenced by several factors as they have diverse background and ideology (*India International* 116). Badal Sircar, another distinguished playwright, discourses in this connection:

> The people in action are people like us, but also different from us, detached from us. They did not come through the same doors that we

> used, and they would go out by a different way when the event would be over. Even now, they are not aware of our presence, or are pretending that they are not – which means that are ignoring us, that we are useless to them. But at the same time we *know* that we are not useless; whatever they are doing, they are doing for our sake. Without us, *they* would be useless (12).

The viewers may or may not affect the enactment on the stage. One can turn the page back but not the performance. The performance on the stage has a series of enactments at its back – the replications of dialogues, expressions, gesticulations, mapping the space, etc. during run through. Though the viewers come to the theatre prepared to be illuded, the playwright has persistently to be watchful of the carefully chosen words and the challenge of choosing it because the play is mostly written to be performed and it has to converse through the fourth wall. Sengupta elaborates it:

> The overarching challenge to the playwright is that the play must work on stage. The transfer from page to performance requires that the writer be clear about the central aspect of theatre. Unlike other performing arts, where the aesthetics of the form is paramount, a dramatic script relies heavily on the spoken word. It is this spoken word that takes us into the private thoughts and emotions of characters who are apparently not performing for us, who are leading their lives in their different ways while we, the audience, watch and hear them through a peephole, a window, a pair of binoculars. We are, in a sense, voyeurs (*India International* 115).

The pronounced word itself is not enough and also not anassurance of fruitful communication of the message/idea to the audience and the dramatist has to remain vigilant, during the process of writing the play, concerning the how of it. Sengupta elaborates it further:

> I must remember not only the inherent cogency of my writing, but must be aware, always, that my play is meant for performance, that I must be conscious of the logic and the laws of the stage. I must also be aware that my writing will be conveyed to an audience through a 'middleman'; that it will go through another and a different creative process through the theatre director. Perhaps the most important element that I must be mindful of is that a dramatic narrative has a direct impact on an audience with a powerful and potential impetus for action. A play also has another important dimension to its impact in performance: its pages cannot be turned back. The playwright cannot be too nuanced or subtle for a motley audience (*India International* 114).

In *Thus Spake Shoorpanakha,* the dramatist communicates, in addition to words, expressions and gestures, through the costume and the set – the restroom (which remains before the eyes of the public to be seen and felt) is used for costume change and, when the characters come out of that, how s/he is changed in mood and expression. "I realised," Sengupta emphasises in an interview, "how important it was to give specific tones and speech patterns to characters so that they do not speak the same way, so that their thinking itself is particular to them. This distinctness makes for sharpness in character delineation" (*Asian Theatre* 87) The audience takes it for granted that every time the restroom is used for costume, the person that comes out of it is a changed man – either a contemporary wo/man or Shoorpanakha/Shakuni. "It's a recognition game," Sircar asserts, and the playwright "knows the man he has put in his play as a character, the director recognises the man and helps the performer to recognise him, the performer copies the man in his performance so that the spectator can also recognise him" (17).

Shakuni wanted revenge, as he asserts, "[h]ot...bloody...fanged revenge" (*Thus Spake* 262). He calls himself "an illusionist," like Shoorpanakha (*Thus Spake* 263). His dispute, however, was the marriage of his sister to a blind king: "They brought her ceremoniously...grandly...for a royal wedding...a grand royal wedding...to be married to a...blind man..." (*Thus Spake* 264). He did nothing but "ranted and raved" (*Thus Spake* 265). Out of anger, he supplements, his sister also blindfolded herself. The dialogue between Man (Shakuni) and Woman (Shoorpanakha), at this point, is worth observing:

MAN: You? Shoorpanakha? The demoness?

WOMAN: I belong to the mighty asura clan.

MAN: And you know all the tricks. You use beauty, the illusion of beauty, don't you, to trap all those poor fools? Like that purple flower with an exotic Latin name...and then when they get close they smell the garlic. And the blood of the men you have gorged on.

WOMAN: How dare you say this to me?

MAN: What do you have to be angry about, ogress? You tried to seduce a married man...he repulsed you. So what? You could always have tried your art on other married fools.

WOMAN: I fell in love with him, don't you see? I was all open to him...like the earth receiving the rain. And he...he was entranced too. He talked to me as if...as if he needed all those arguments...about respectability and fucking commitment...to keep away from me. Otherwise if I so much as touched his elbow, he would crumple into my arm and suck the breath out through my lips.

The MAN snorts.

MAN: Why don't you tell the truth? Yu lusted for him. You wanted sex with him.

WOMAN: Yes. I did. Is that wrong?

Pause.

WOMAN: But then something strange happened. Has it happened to you? You think of somebody all the time...all the bloody time...while you are working ... eating ... travelling...even when you are asleep...And then it's not just sex anymore. It's... (*Softly.*) it's as if I am dissolved in him, his body outlines mine, his fingertips awaken everything I touch.

Pause

WOMAN: Your sister lost only her sight. I lost myself...I lost me.

Pause.

WOMAN: Can't you see? Because I love him...I've forgotten how he hurt me. And I...(*Softly.*) I can't hurt anyone anymore. I have lost the need to hurt...

MAN: For god's sake, you sound like a bloody saint.

WOMAN: Oh, ... you. Do you have to classify me? ... (*Wearily.*) I am a woman, don't you understand? A woman. Not a saint. Not a whore. Not just a mother, a sister, a daughter. I am a woman. (*Thus Spake* 265-67)

This interchange between Shoorpanakha and Shakuni points at numerous aspects of myths that have never been, perhaps, acknowledged or reconnoitered but represented in the play by Poile Sengupta. Shoorpanakha, though she admits to be a part of 'mighty asura clan,' objects to be called a 'demoness' or 'ogress'. The audience also witnesses how, being 'lost' in love, she expresses her love and infatuation. Another significant point that the viewers note is her protest against not being acknowledged as a woman. But a more important point is her statement 'I can't hurt anyone anymore. I have lost the need to hurt' which is in contradiction to her later behaviour when she picks up the suitcase carrying explosives and almost starts moving for another disasterof present-day mankind. Thus, the audience notes, her character is untrustworthy and one cannot whollyapprove with what she says about the incident that took place between her and the two brothers, and the depth and dignity of her expressed love, thus, becomes doubtful.

Shakuni, to return to the 'illusionist', remained immersed in making plots to retaliate the wrongs done to his sister and, indirectly to him. He asserts, "They were my nephews, yes...all of them. But when plotting revenge, nothing else is important ... not my nephews ... not me ... Finally ... not even my sister ... I wanted to turn everything to dust. Dust and ashes" (*Thus Spake* 269).So he began the war between the brothers, between the teacher and the taught, and between friends. He becomes the vehicle of the "mother of all wars" (*Thus Spake* 269). The audience, then, comes to know the earlier story of Shakuni – of how he, along with his brothers, was taken a captive and was cast into a prison. His brothers would give him their shareof food to let Shakuni live and take revenge. His brothers died one by one and when he was surprisingly released, he found everyone busy with the arrangements for his sister's marriage with one of the clans that imprisoned him and his brothers. This part of the play, the audience knows, is not a part of the myth in *Mahabharata* and hence they do not have belief in the character. In this way, the character of Shakuni has uncertaingenuineness and cannot be taken as anhonest representative of the mythical tale. The reality, as the dramatist has successfully offered in the play, is that he is the one who has brought the suitcase having explosives in it for a mass destruction. He is "the villain ... the sly, cunning manipulator" (*Thus Spake* 274).

Performativity and performance are also enacted in a play not only through words, expressions or gestures, but also through pauses and silences. Such a technique is used to reveal the subtext or the unspoken interaction between the characters on the page or stage. Johm Lutterbie maintains, "Silence, in a pure state, is absolute absence, and therefore beyond representation; it can be thought of only as a space defining the interface of opposites" (468). Pauses, Lutterbie explains, are "viewed as transparent, permitting an empathy between the characters and the audience" (474). The playwright argues in this connection:

> Apart from the words, however, theatre uses movement and gesture and also, paradoxically, silence as elements of communication. In fact, among all forms of literature and the performing arts, it is theatre that uses silence as a significant, powerful and effective device (*India International* 119).

The play is full of pauses and silences with pregnant connotations. Look at this short dialogue:

WOMAN: I better warn you. I have high connections.

Silence.

WOMAN: One of my brothers … my stepbrother actually … is rich enough to buy up all the Middle East.

Pause.

WOMAN: And my brother, who will do anything for me, is as … as strong and … and as powerful as ten men …

Silence.

Man does neither speak nor respond here as if he is either a patient listener or a person being silenced after the intimidations. He is, in a way, in the process of being othered and is being turned into a subaltern. Another significant point to note here is the use of ellipses. Woman, it seems, flounders for words to threaten Man and, during the process, represents her mind or, in other words, her character. The play is full of such pregnant ellipses, pauses and silences that fill the gap between the spoken words, and adds to the glimmering performative representation of the characters, their mind, and their postmodern inability, if we dare to say so, to express well through words. It can be inferred here that when language is incapable of containing the subject, silence/pause is used to capture the realm of the unpresentable which is a landscape of the psyche. The images so created become, Lutterbie argues, "the site of gestation, of creation and transformation, of preparing to give birth" (474).

The play keeps moving between past and present. The entire play takes place at the airport but the characters keep going to their primeval times through their memory lanes and remember their past and how they had been ostracized and subdued to the social margin and, overlooked entirely after their roles got completed in the scheme of things. The focus of the playwright to interlace varied stories into a single one is to demonstrate how the society, then and now, relegates those people to marginality who become vehicles in overturning the storylines and bring tragedy to humankind. Shoorpanakha and Shakuni are heroes of evil, as the myths go, who, by their evil strategies, bring twists to the otherwise linear stories and intensify the climax leading to tragic events that bring carnage. Shashi Deshpande, in the"Introduction" to *Women Centre Stage* writes:

> The myths have been upturned very casually, with no attempt at solemnity, yet very effectively. And both these villains show us another side of themselves, without shedding their murky pasts. They are victim as well as vengeance seekers. And while seeming to replay the roles allotted

to them by history, they struggle to redeem themselves and do so in the end (xiii).

Though the playwright seems to take sides of these two characters in the narrative, she fails to shun the truth that evil minds seldom change and, thus, the contemporary Shoorpanakha and Shakuni are represented to become vehicles in bringing devastation and human fatality toward the end of the play. Though they leave the briefcase having explosives at the airport, this representation is once again unconvincing as the audience remains apprehensive whether the bomb explodes or not.

It would not be wrong to suggest here that a play is no longer an entity in itself. Its intended meaning may be misunderstood or partially understood by the audience. The audience remains fully emancipated even when the playwright works toward some specific idea with the help of spectacles on the stage. A play becomes a "potential mediator" for the contemporary reader/audience that inspires the "non-spectacular encounters" and allows him to interpret the play in numberless ways (Pujante 169). To sum up, it would be in place to quote Pujante that "plays are no longer locked inside the realm of their own aura, as the focus has been shifted to the role of the audience and the relational context of the event. Theatrical events have stopped being finished, invariable objects—they have become unique entities subject to constant change" (169).

Works Cited

Deshpande, Shashi. "Introduction". *Women Centre Stage: The Dramatist and the Play* by Poile Sengupta. Routledge, 2010.

Fludernik, Monika. "Consciousness in Drama: A Cognitive Approach," *Dramatic Minds: Performance, Cognition, and the Representation of Interiority,* edited by Werner Huber *et al.,* Peter Lang, 2015, pp. 21-41.

Kalhat, Javier. "Varieties of Representation". *Philosophy,* vol. 91, no. 355, January 2016, pp. 15-37. JSTOR, http://www.jstor.org/stable/10.2307/26419247.

Lutterbie, John. "Subjects of Silence." *Theatre Journal,* vol. 40, no. 4, Dec. 1988, pp. 468-81. JSTOR, http://www.jstor.org/stable/3207889.

Phelan, Peggy. *Unmarked: The Politics of Performance.* Routledge, 1993.

Prendergast, Christopher. *The Triangle of Representation.* Columbia UP, 2000.

Pujante, Belen Tortosa. "Performative Contexts in Contemporary Theatre: Towards the Emancipation of the Relational Space." *Context in Literary and Cultural Studies,* edited by Jakob Ladegaard and Jakob Gaardbo, UCL P, 2019, pp. 156-71.

Ranciere, Jacques. *The Emancipated Spectator.* Verso, 2008.

Reinelt, Janelle. "Introduction". *Key Words: Journal of Cultural Materialism,* 2017, no. 15, pp. 9-22. JSTOR, http://www.jstor.org/stable/26920433.

Savage, Roger. "Introducing Drama." *Edinburgh Introduction to Studying English Literature,* edited by Dermot Cavanagh, Edinburgh UP, 2010, pp. 161-170.

Schechner, Richard. "Behavior, Performance, and Performance Space". *Perspecta,* vol. 26, 1990, pp. 97-102. JSTOR, http://www.jstor.org/stable/1567156.

---. "Drama, Script, Theatre, and Performance". *The Drama Review: TDR,* vol. 17, no. 3, Sept. 1973, pp. 5-36. JSTOR, http://www.jstor.org/stable/1144841.

---. "Performance Studies: The Broad Spectrum Approach". *TDR,* vol. 32, no. 3, autumn 1988, pp. 4-6. JSTOR, http://www.jstor.org/stable/1145899.

Sengupta, Poile. "Theatre: A Playwright's Illusion". *India International Centre Quarterly,* vol. 41, no. 2, autumn 2014, pp. 113-20. JSTOR, http://www.jstor.org/stable/24390754.

---. *Thus Spake Shoorpanakha: So Said Shakuni* in *Women Centre Stage: The Dramatist and the Play.* Routledge, 2010.

Sengupta, Poile, and Anita Singh. "An Interview with Poile Sengupta". *Asian Theatre Journal,* vol. 29, no. 1, spring 2012, pp. 78-88. JSTOR, http://www.jstor.org/stable/23359545.

Sircar, Badal. *The Changing Language of Theatre.* Indian Council for Cultural Relations, 1982.

States, Bert O. "Performance as Metaphor". *Theatre Journal,* March 1996, vol. 48, no. 1, pp. 1-26. JSTOR, http://www.jstor.org/stable/3208711.

Zettelmann, Eva. "Drama and the Representation of Fictional Minds." Werner Huber *et al,* pp. 43-59.

Index

F

G

H

I

J

K

L

N

O

P